The Busy Homeschool Mom's Guide™ to
Daylight

Other Books By Heidi St. John

The Busy Homeschool Mom's Guide to Romance
Nurturing Your Marriage Through the Homeschool Years

Words Along the Way - A Busy Mom's Journal

What I love about Heidi St. John is she is transparent, relatable and hilarious to boot. Trust me, she's been reading your mail, and you'll be glad she did. Heidi understands the challenges facing the Christian woman who is a wife, mother and homeschooler. And she doesn't lower the bar for us in anyway; but lifts up our eyes to the One who is our help. This is how to be God-empowered and God-graced in your ministry to your family. Heidi St. John's Guide to Daylight will pull up the blinds in the darkest corners of your harried, frazzled life and let the Son shine in.

Debra Bell, AUTHOR
*THE ULTIMATE GUIDE TO HOMESCHOOLING
AND THE ULTIMATE HOMESCHOOL PLANNING SYSTEM*

Heidi St John's newest book, *The Busy Homeschool Mom's Guide to Daylight*, offers renewed hope for busy moms who may sometimes be overwhelmed with all that needs to be done every day. Honest, funny, candid and poignant, Heidi's writing always hits home with a helping hand from someone who has already been there and learned the ins and outs.

Jane Claire Lambert, AUTHOR
FIVE IN A ROW

Heidi St. John knows how to meet you where you live – in your kitchen, in the car, even in your closet. It's clear that Heidi has a plan for when things don't go as planned. She teaches us how to be adaptable, how to solve problems, how to laugh at ourselves, and how to get the most out of our homeschool experience. Best of all, Heidi gently reminds us not to feel inadequate when other moms seem to have it all together. You will be a more confident homeschool mom after you read this book.

Elizabeth Smith, SPEAKER
WIFE OF HSLDA PRESIDENT MIKE SMITH

Here it is! A realistic, doable, self-effacing solution to the 'I am not organized enough to homeschool' excuse. If organization has delayed take off on your homeschool adventure, buckle your seat belt. You have been cleared for departure!

Rachael Carman, AUTHOR
HOW TO HAVE A H.E.A.R.T. FOR YOUR KIDS

Managing your day is important, but you won't succeed unless able to manage yourself, first. You can do it. Stick around—Heidi will take you by the hand and lead you down a quiet journey of peaceful transformation as you lean on the Master Manager Himself.

Gena Suarez, PUBLISHER
THE OLD SCHOOLHOUSE® MAGAZINE

The Busy Homeschool Mom's Guide™ to

Daylight

Managing Your Days

Through the Homeschool Years

Heidi St. John

You can do this!

Heidi St. John

Mt 19:26

Real Life

PRESS

The Busy Homeschool Mom's Guide™to Daylight:
Managing Your Days Through the Homeschool Years

Published by Real Life Press
Vancouver, Washington

©2012, By Heidi St. John

Photos by carolynsmithphotography.com ©2012 All rights reserved.
Costume and set design: Makayla Estoos & Savannah St. John
Cover graphic design: Jay St. John & Michael Bozeman

All inquiries should be addressed to:
Heidi St. John
% First Class Homeschool Ministries
1400 NE 136th Avenue
Vancouver, WA 98684
email: heidi@fchm.org
www.heidistjohn.com
www.firstclasshomeschool.org

Printed in the United States of America
ISBN 978-0-9844323-1-8

To every busy homeschool mom who has ever been mistaken for a person with supernatural patience or who wanted to call a substitute teacher for the day:

You deserve much affirmation for the immeasurable investment you are making each day as a wife, mother and teacher. You are shaping history while you teach it.

I hope this book encourages you to wisely use every precious moment of daylight you have been given to influence and nurture your children in the ways of the Lord.

The homeschool years go by so fast—

Enjoy them!

Contents

FOREWORD

"What do you think is the hardest part of homeschooling?" the young mom asked after I finished speaking at a conference on the West Coast.

I hesitated for just a few seconds before answering her, as I quickly scrolled through our 21 years of homeschooling in my mind's eye. The state superintendent of education had threatened me with jail when Joe and I began homeschooling in 1984. What a harrowing experience that was! But that wasn't the hardest part of homeschooling.

For eight years our family had fought for the rights of South Carolina homeschoolers in the legislature, the judicial system, and in the court of public opinion. Those were frightening and unsettling times. But that wasn't the hardest part of homeschooling.

Joe and I didn't know another homeschooling family in the entire world when we began teaching our children at home. We were ostracized by close friends, neighbors, church members, and relatives.   But that wasn't the hardest part of homeschooling.

The hardest part of homeschooling was the constant pressure I felt for my children's welfare. As a homeschooling mother, I wanted the very best for Ty, John, and Lizzy. I aspired for them to have a solid, invigorating education that would prepare them for college, career, and life in general. I wanted them to be happy. I longed for them to love our family. I desired for them to develop their strengths and have a sense of calling. And most of all, I yearned for them to know God.

But, in the wee hours of the morning, I constantly woke up worrying that instead of blessing my children through homeschooling, I was actually ruining them. During those 2:00 a.m. panic attacks, I fretted over socialization. I agonized over the daunting task of preparing them for college and career. I wondered if they would resent having been homeschooled when they grew up. I stressed over how I would ever teach algebra, physics, and Spanish (the boys were six and four at the time). And as I worried and stressed and fretted, deep down I knew that I was totally inadequate for the monumental task at hand.

What do you think is the hardest part of the homeschooling? Have you ever been overwhelmed by its demands? Have you ever been tempted to throw in the towel and put your children on that bright yellow school bus that stops right outside your door every morning? If so, you are not alone!

In *The Busy Homeschool Mom's Guide to Daylight*, Heidi St. John pulls back the curtain on her own life and lets us peek in. In her inimitable style, she discusses frankly and honestly the things that plague us the most as homeschooling moms. And she offers hope, inspiration, and practical solutions.

But what Heidi does best is to beckon us to fall on our knees and sit at the feet of Jesus. She calls us to seek God honestly and fervently in the midst of our weaknesses, our failures, and trials. She gently admonishes us to replace our fears with faith—and to refuse to grow weary in well-doing. And she reminds us of why we decided to homeschool in the first place.

How I wish I could have held this little volume in my hands when I was homeschooling! I pray that the Lord will encourage and inspire you as you read *The Busy Homeschool Mom's Guide to Daylight*.

A fellow laborer in Christ,

Zan Tyler
Director of Apologia Press
Speaker/Author of
7 Tools for Cultivating Your Child's Potential
www.apologia.com

ACKNOWLEDGEMENTS

I praise the Lord every day for the special people who have contributed in big and small ways to this book.

My husband, Jay St. John is the most incredible man I have ever known. Thank you, Jay, for all you have done to see this book in print—and for being the man I get to write about! Your wisdom, strength of character and love bless us all every day.

To Savannah, Sierra, Skylar, Spencer, Summer, Sydney and Saylor Jane —you are such a delight to your dad and me! Thank you for filling our lives with joy and for embracing the adventure we are on together. We love you!

To our dear friends Steve and Jane Lambert: Thank you for your honest advice and prayerful encouragement. Because of your example, I am learning to look for God in unexpected places.

Every mom should have several great go-to girlfriends. I am blessed that a few of mine took the time to help me write another book on top of everything else they do! To Patty Slack Marcy Wilde, Tandy Hogate and my mom-in-love, Jerry St. John, thank you for patiently wading through hundreds of typos and apostrophe catastrophes; To Makayla Estoos and Carolyn Smith, you're amazing! Thank you for once again bringing "That Girl" to life with wonderful flair and creativity.

I sent out a few pleas for help on Facebook this past year and they were answered by some wonderful moms. Thank you to everyone who sent in your family schedule and who helped me with initial reviews for this book. Many moms will benefit from your willingness to share a glimpse into your homeschool day!

Jay and I greatly appreciate our "other" family—the friends we serve alongside at First Class Homeschool Ministries. We love and appreciate your hearts for ministering to the homeschool community! It's our privilege to get to hang out with you and be part of your lives.

Thanks to the folks at Main Street Station in Battle Ground, Washington for allowing Makayla and I to raid your store for fun vintage props. We'll be back!

And finally, I want to thank my Mom, for teaching me to manage my own daylight well. I am a better mom because of you. Thanks for putting up with all seven of us—and for making those spinning chore charts with the clothespin people. It took a while, but I finally get it. I love you!

First Things First

KEEPING YOUR FAMILY YOUR TOP PRIORITY

*T*his morning, I was standing in my bathroom putting makeup on ... our third grader next to me doing her math, "Mom, what is 'greater than' again?" ... first grader sitting next to the shower door, "Mom, I wrote my 'S' backward again!" ... discover the baby crawling out of the room with a washcloth in her mouth ... fifth grader calls from kitchen table, "Mom! I can't find my grammar book!" (*sigh*) ...ninth grader comes in and asks if he can take a break (it's only 9 a.m.) ... and, after 45 minutes, I have one eye done. 9 a.m. and I was behind the eight ball. As I looked at my third grader, she smiled at me. "Mommy?"

"Yes?"

"You only have one eye fancy."

Can you relate?

Homeschooling is a tall order. It can seem overwhelming. And at times, it is. I know. As a homeschool mom of seven children, I have had my moments. Believe me. Just last week I was begging my sweet husband to watch the kids for an hour so that I could go sit in the car and listen to, well, nothing.

If you are at the end of your homeschool rope, tie a knot and hang on!

Truth be told, over the past fourteen years, I have wanted to throw the homeschool towel in on numerous occasions. I confess, I've often looked at that big yellow school bus as it passed by my front yard with longing in my eyes. I've wondered what it would be like to put my kids on that bus—just for the day—and walk back inside to a quiet house. Yes, I have fantasized about enjoying my morning tea before it got cold or finishing a thought before it was interrupted. I dare say I'm not alone in my fantasyland either, because I've spoken to many moms over the years who have had that exact same dream from time to time. It's okay. It's normal. There is not a mom on the planet who has not wondered on occasion what in the world she got herself into. Homeschool moms are no different.

So, if you are at the end of your homeschool rope, tie a knot and hang on! We're going to talk about some very practical ways to manage the daytime hours in your home so that you can make the most of the precious years God has given you with your children. But first, we've got to be willing to lay down our expectations and ask the Lord to reveal His heart for our homeschool. We've got to be honest about where we are, why we're homeschooling and what's at stake. We've got to surrender our hearts to find His heart.

In the surrender of laying our burdens at His feet, we find peace and even (dare I say it?) rest!

Why? Because His yoke is easy, and His burden is light. If God has called you to homeschool—and since you're reading this, I'm assuming He has—then He has already equipped you with everything you need to get the job done.

Managing your day, after all, is really just about learning to manage yourself.

Managing your day, after all, is really just about learning to manage yourself. But before you can do that, you've got to make sure your priorities are in order.

First Things First - Making Your Marriage the Priority Relationship at Home

Wonder Twin Powers ... ACTIVATE!

Ever heard this phrase? Okay, I know I am dating myself just by writing it at all ... but the analogy for marriage is so good, I'm willing to risk it! In case you don't remember, the Wonder Twins were part of the 70's cartoon craze, and I'll admit I watched them. Religiously. There. Now you know.

I'm sure you're wondering where I'm going with this, but trust me: I'm going to make a point with the Wonder Twins. It might be the only redeeming thing to come out of all those wasted hours watching them! However, you will need a little history so allow me to bring you up to speed on these super heroes of long ago.

According to Hannah-Barbera, the Wonder Twins had amazing superpowers. These powers were activated when they touched each other and spoke the phrase, "Wonder Twin Powers, Activate!" Hey, it was cool when I was ten.

Now as nice as that sounds, it wasn't enough just to say the phrase. Physical contact was also required. If the Wonder Twins were out of reach of each other, they were unable to activate their powers.

You see, without being connected to each other in two very crucial ways, they were just like ordinary people, and Swamp Monster could beat them. Still wondering how this applies? Keep reading …

My husband and I have a little Wonder Twin joke. Whenever we feel depleted or unable to function effectively as a team, it's usually because, like the Wonder Twins, we're out of reach of each other in one or both of the ways that the dynamic duo could not survive without.

Emotional Distance

I wrote an entire book dedicated to this topic so I won't belabor it here … but it bears repeating that when it comes to relationships within your home, your marriage should be the first relationship you nurture. We women are, as a general rule, emotional by nature. Many marriages suffer and fail because, left untended, emotional distance between the couple cannot be bridged. Conflict is never fun. Many moms would rather send "signals" to their husbands to get their point across than broach an uncomfortable topic. But here's the thing: your husband can't be expected to address a problem that he knows nothing about!

Occasionally, it's my husband who is battling some sort of inner turmoil. Maybe it's a big decision that's weighing on his mind. Things at work might be frustrating or discouraging. When he was pastoring, there would be times he would come home from the church and go straight to our room—leaving me to wonder what was wrong and feeling helpless to do anything about it. Sound familiar?

God has created marriage so that we might come together as husband and wife ... a "dynamic duo" for the Kingdom, if you will ... and join God in the work He is already doing. The enemy of our soul knows full well that if he can create a little distance between you and your husband, it will go a long way in undermining your marriage.

It's amazing how lack of communication can affect the relationship between a husband and wife. Oftentimes I'm frustrated with how disorganized and chaotic our days seem, when a simple conversation with my husband would reveal a side of our problem I had failed to discern before.

Busy homeschool mom, communicate with your husband. Let him in to those places that are uncomfortable to talk about: lack of organization, fear of failing the kids, discouragement. Your husband can't meet you halfway if he doesn't know what road you're on.

Physical Distance

Another thing we can learn from the Wonder Twins is the fact that it's not enough just to communicate. "Wonder Twin Powers, Activate!" doesn't do them any good if there is not physical contact.

Sometimes, busy moms are too busy to notice the distance that creeps in between a husband and wife simply due to lack of physical intimacy. Being a mom is challenging enough. Adding homeschooling takes it to a whole new level. It's easy to let homeschooling take priority in your life. And it's dangerous, too.

Communicate with your husband. He can't meet you halfway if he doesn't know what road you're on.

As much as you want to learn to manage your day, an even greater responsibility needs to come first: your marriage.

Women, please do NOT neglect the sexual aspect of your marriage. Talk to your husband about it. Ask him to tell you honestly how he feels your marriage is doing in this important area. You might be surprised by the answer you hear.

Think about what attracted you to your husband when you were first married. Ask him what attracted him to you. In *The Busy Homeschool Mom's Guide to Romance*, I wrote about

"That Girl." She's the girl your husband married! She's the one who couldn't wait to romance her husband, to make him dinner, to dress beautifully for him.

You're still "That Girl," busy homeschool mom!—and "That Girl" still needs to be part of your life and marriage.

Nurturing Relationships with Your Kids

"Mom, you're not fun to be around anymore."

Ouch.

These were the words spoken from my teary-eyed nine-year old after I asked the age old question, "What's wrong?" in the middle of a math assignment. It took some time to get the answer out of this tender-hearted child. Things had been tense for weeks but I ignored most of the signs, hoping that, eventually, the kids would adjust to my "new and improved" way of doing things.

It had been about four months since I implemented my new routine, and now I was beginning to hear how what worked for me was not necessarily working for the family. I'm sad to say, it wasn't good news on the relationship front.

As it turned out, I was driving the household a little bit nutty with my hour-by-hour schedule. My "no pain, no gain" attitude was a little hard to deal with every day. But I reasoned and justified away any excuse for a walk to the park or a day off of the schedule by just looking at the sheer amount of work that had to be done to get through a day successfully.

After all, we had so much to do! There was laundry to sort and dishes to wash. Dinner had to be made. And don't forget about schoolwork! I reasoned that it didn't leave much time for relationships outside of the necessary and oh-so-daily character and obedience training.

Let's be known for going to Jesus to seek His priorities before we pencil in our own.

Days turned into weeks, weeks into months. I couldn't remember the last time I baked cookies with the kids or did something that was not related to housework with them for more than five minutes. I was so busy surviving our busy life I was not taking time for the stuff that makes life great!

The fact is, being available to relax with my family just wasn't a priority for me. To be honest, I still struggle with it. My "type A" personality grates against a free afternoon at the park because I worry that the "important" things will be left undone.

But who defines "important?" As our children have grown older, I will confess, my definition of "important" has undergone quite a few changes. I think it's due to the fact that I'm recognizing that the things I worried about as a younger homeschool mom were often the least important things. I wrung my hands and fretted over whether or not there would be "gaps" in the children's education. Prepositions, algebra lessons, writing assignments, and proving my homeschool savvy had become my focus instead.

Jesus tells us what's really important: "Seek first the Kingdom of God and HIS righteousness and all these things will be added to you as well." (Matthew 6:33)

It's so easy to get busy doing the wrong things, isn't it? In fact, sometimes even the right things end up being wrong. I'm not saying you need to ditch your schedule. In fact, the opposite is true! I'm not saying don't do school if you'd rather be playing a rousing game of Sorry™, either.

What I am saying is, "Keep your finger on the pulse of your family!"

Periodically take the time for self evaluation. What's working? What's not working? Are the relationships in your home suffering because of something you are doing that could be changed a bit?

Ask yourself, "When our children are grown, what do I want them to remember about their homeschool days?" My hunch is that you don't want them to remember a hurried, harried, stressed-out mom who was not much more fun than a math assignment!

When our kids graduate from our homeschool (one down, six to go), I want them to remember that their dad and I loved them.

Even on busy days, I hope they remember that we loved them. I don't want them to look back and think of me as a mom who cared more about academics and housework than I did about dreaming with them and enjoying each stage (and phase!) of their lives.

The days go by so fast. Are you enjoying them?

Seeing the Bigger Picture

Most moms I know are always trying to learn how to make the most of the precious daylight hours, but there is a bigger picture we need to keep in focus. As we talk about planning our day, let's keep this in mind. Time is a gift, and so are the children God has given us to raise. So try this: when you think of homeschooling, scheduling, housework and dishes, ask the Lord to give you His perspective. Everything else falls into place when we know we're doing what He's asked first.

I truly believe that Christian homeschooling is nothing short of a "God thing." Apart from His leading, we could never do it. Do you want to learn about His power being perfected in weakness? Become a homeschool mom. Whether you are an accidental homeschooler like me, or you have always known you would homeschool, the challenge that home education provides us with is fertile soil in which to dig deep into the truths of God's Word—and to find out just how powerful He really is.

> Do you want to learn about His power being perfected in weakness? Become a homeschool mom.

That's what homeschooling is teaching me, and I hope to pass some of what I'm learning on to other busy homeschool moms. My hope is that you find encouragement in the pages of this book. I pray that by the time you are done reading it, whether you're at the beginning of your journey or a homeschool veteran, you'll feel a little bit lighter and more confident that "He who has begun a good work in you will see it through to completion". (Philippians 1:6)

Busy homeschool moms, let's be known for going to Jesus to seek His priorities before we pencil in our own. He will help us maintain a healthy balance throughout the homeschool years.

No, it's not always easy, but it's a journey worth taking! It's the hardest, best thing you'll ever do with your children. So come on, mom! Jump in with me and let's seek God's heart together as we get intentional about how we spend our days.

There's no time to lose! After all, we're burnin' daylight!

CHAPTER 1

Intentional Daylight

WHY YOU NEED A POA, ASAP

Seek the LORD and his strength,
seek his face continually.
~ 1 Chronicles 16:11

"Good Morning, Portland! It's 6:45 a.m. and traffic into downtown is at a virtual standstill this morning ... plan on taking an alternate route if you want to avoid the mess on I-5 today ..." The voice of a local radio station personality woke me from a deep sleep and I began to regret putting my alarm clock clear across the room. Was it already time to get up? Time to try this homeschool "thing" again? Time to see exactly how much resolve I could muster up to face another day?

Daylight. It had come back again.

I stumbled to the alarm clock and shut it off. 6:45 a.m. and already, I was feeling behind. Unanswered emails taunted me from my computer (a desktop, by the way). And there on my side table sat a devotional book that I had promised to read three weeks ago. It was looking rather dusty. As I made my way to the shower, I picked the book up, blew off the dust and placed it back on a shelf where it wouldn't remind me of all the things I wished I was doing, but wasn't.

As I walked past the dresser mirror, I caught a glimpse of a pregnant woman I barely recognized. "Whoever you are, you better get a grip," I mused. I toyed with the idea of letting the kids sleep in—for my sake. I wasn't ready to face the day. Why was it so hard? I had been homeschooling for about a year and a half, and it was getting the better of me. This was certainly NOT what I had envisioned when the Lord so clearly changed my heart and directed my husband and me to bring our oldest daughter home from school to begin the journey of homeschooling.

I was homeschooling all right—but that was it. The rest of my life was unraveling.

My kids didn't look like the ones that graced the covers of those homeschool magazines. It seemed that just when I got something down in one area of the house, another would need improving.

What about that mom I met at the

homeschool convention this past June? I wondered how she was still breathing—she had something like nineteen kids and I suddenly felt lazy for only having three!

There was so much to do. Laundry called my name from several hampers in the house. I had no idea what I was going to do for dinner, and forget about all the paperwork that was piling up in the office—bills to pay, forms to fill out. I was homeschooling all right—but that was it. The rest of my life was unraveling.

I wondered if there was a better way to homeschool, less stressful and more joyful. Less burdensome. More life giving. Often I found myself giving comfort to another mom when I felt in my spirit that I didn't have much to offer. My time with the Lord was suffering terribly, and in my heart, I knew there had to be a better way. I had heard that His yoke was easy, but I felt I had yet to experience it.

Something had to give. As I looked around my bedroom that morning, I made a decision. A monumental decision. Here it is:

> In the interest of self-preservation, I decided to skip school for the day.

Can I get a witness?

After a few more moments of relative peace and quiet and after savoring my morning cup of tea, I decided to go to the grocery store to clear my head. So I packed up the toddler, and put my two older girls in the car. We headed into town even though I was feeling slightly guilty for skipping school. I figured the break would do me good however, and it was certainly better than the alternative, which may or may not have involved in-patient therapy!

It was about 10:30 a.m. when we arrived at the grocery store.

In hindsight, I think staying home might have been a better idea.

Yes, I'm Just That Crazy

"Oh, I could NEVER do that!"

This was the wide-eyed response of the grocery store cashier after she casually asked the children if they were taking a "sick" day from school. The moment my children told her they were homeschooled, it became obvious by the look in her eyes that she thought I was perfectly insane.

"You must have a whole lot more patience than me!" she stammered, "Because I would have to be shipped off to the funny farm if I couldn't put my kids in school! I don't know how you people do it! How old are you? You must be exhausted! Well, good luck! ... and thanks for shopping with us today!"

Now, maybe it was the fact that I was seven months pregnant with our fourth child, or maybe it was the knowledge that I was going home to a messy kitchen complete with school books, pencils, markers and paper all over the kitchen table, I don't know. But for some reason, her remarks stung more than they usually would.

The foundation and power of homeschooling is found in the quiet resolve of two parents who are committed to teaching their children to be fully devoted, mature followers of Jesus Christ.

It wasn't like I had never heard them before, but this time—this time I wanted to drop my bag of canned goods right there on the floor and give her the what for. I don't know what stopped me, frankly. I like to think that I was just trying not to give other homeschool moms a bad reputation. Trust me, it would have stuck.

I managed a half-smile and said something to the effect of not having as much patience as she thought and quickly left the store.

"NO, *I don't* have the patience of Job," I muttered. It's *not about patience.* If it was, I would have quit a long time ago.

A Crucial Component to Success in Homeschooling

Can you relate to being mistaken for a mom with supernatural patience? I imagine you can. But most homeschooling moms know the truth about patience being a prerequisite for homeschooling. In fact, any homeschool mom who has been at it for more than five minutes will tell you that patience has nothing to do with it.

Longevity in homeschooling is the result of resolve and obedience; it's certainly *not* about patience! It's about knowing *why* we're homeschooling instead of just *how*. Spirit-led homeschooling brings with it a quiet confidence that comes from knowing that even on days when I don't feel like I've been successful at all, God's got my back.

After all, they were His kids before they were mine. He knit each one together with the foreknowledge that I would be homeschooling them. His plan for them is vastly more important than my dinner plans or fancy scheduling.

Do you believe it? You need to, because God wants to work

in your heart as you trust Him to finish the work He has begun in you through the process of homeschooling.

The Goal of Education

Do you remember when you were in school? Chances are you do. Many, if not most of the moms who are currently homeschooling were not homeschooled themselves. We attended school away from home—where we were discipled by our teacher. We don't often think of education this way, but at the end of the day, education is all about discipleship.

Discipleship is the goal of education.

Discipleship is the goal of education. Christian homeschooling should not simply be about teaching the ABC's. Yes, academics are an essential component of homeschooling, but the foundation and power of homeschooling is found in the quiet resolve of two parents who are committed to teaching their children to be fully devoted, mature followers of Jesus Christ.

That comes first.

Understanding this is a crucial component to successful homeschooling. It's the key that unlocks the door of longevity in home education.

The truth is that the best schedule and most efficiently run home won't keep you from burning out if you don't know why you're doing what you're doing.

So let me just ask you.

Busy homeschool mom, why are you homeschooling? Most moms I know would never, not in a million years, take on homeschooling if they were not driven by something. What's driving you?

Your answer to this question will define your homeschool journey. Keeping the heart of homeschooling alive with a desire to truly impart wisdom (not just knowledge) to your children will help keep you going when you watch other moms put their kids on the school bus and head out for a cup of coffee. Once you truly know why you're homeschooling, you can begin to create a plan that will help you make the most of the homeschool years—one day at a time.

Creating a P.O.A.

Days go by so fast, don't they? When our children were all little, it amazed me at how quickly the daylight hours came and went. Some days I was lucky just to get dressed before

Jay came home from work! Sure, math was done. But dinner? Forget it. As a young homeschool mom, I was experiencing a learning curve that I had not anticipated. I had resolve, but I still felt that I was not managing my time as well as I could.

As the days turned into months, I learned that resolve wasn't all I would need if our family was going to thrive (not just survive) during the homeschool years. If you're going to be successful at homeschooling long term and reap the rewards that come from schooling your children all the way through high school, you've got to get some basic steps in place to secure your footing.

You need a Plan Of Action—a P.O.A., if you will, and you need one A.S.A.P.

And it Worked! ... For A While.

When I was a new homeschool mom, I had a plan. Granted, it was a little bit rough around the edges, but it was a plan nonetheless, and I was eager to implement it. In mid-summer, I attended my very first homeschool convention. While there, I did what many new homeschool moms do: I bought the homeschool farm. I bought a wonderful curriculum—complete with an answer key for second grade math—and took it home to show the kids.

Soon after my curriculum was purchased I bought a book on scheduling. Then, I set to work making our family room into a school room.

Rearranging the furniture in the family room was challenging, but I managed to do it with the help of our two oldest girls. We turned that family room into a classroom that even my third grade teacher would have appreciated! I put phonics charts on the walls, a write-on calendar near the bookshelf and even found two little desks that were exactly like the desks I had in grade school.

Looking back, I realize why it was so important to me to start out this way. I wanted everyone to see that I was serious about homeschooling! Since I had never envisioned myself as a homeschool mom, it seemed reasonable to replicate my classroom experience at home. At least it was a good place to start. We got out our schoolbooks and we did school in the schoolroom with a school calendar and a school clock. We had a school-at-home mindset.

And it worked.

For a while.

Yes, I had a plan. But after a few months, I had

to admit: my planned days were not going like I had envisioned at all. The kids usually ended up at the kitchen table for school because, as it turned out, I needed to be in the kitchen during school time! To my surprise, my regular homeschool day looked very much like my days had always been, except I had added "teacher" to my list of titles.

My well-intentioned plan of spending our days in a home classroom wasn't working, since we spent most of our time in the kitchen or on the living room couch.

It was time to make a change.

And so began the first of several changes that I would make that year in order to adjust to the realities of life. Over the years, I've made many plans. Some of them have worked for me long term, and some have been only for a season. You see, this is a very important concept for homeschool moms to grasp: *The key to successful planning is understanding that even the best plans need to be flexible.*

Successful homeschoolers plan for seasons of life.

Planning for Seasons of Life

Have you ever noticed that there is an ebb and flow to homeschooling? That's because life isn't static. If your life was static, you wouldn't be living at all! Life is constantly changing. Successful homeschool moms—especially the busy ones—learn how to navigate through those changes.

Like seasons in creation, life has seasons. For example, there are seasons of want and seasons of plenty; seasons of rest and seasons of productivity; some seasons are joyful, and others painful. Whatever the season I find myself in, it's comforting to know that God is there, too.

When I began writing this book, I was in a very special season of life myself; the season of having a newborn baby at home. Little baby Saylor arrived in early December of 2010. What that meant for me (and it took me years to surrender to this idea) is that I simply could not do the type of schooling that I truly love, which is very hands-on, with an infant in the house. As much as I love notebooking and lap booking, it took a backseat while Saylor was tiny.

In fact, I will confess, that when I have newborns at home we usually simplify our homeschooling. I keep up by using workbooks rather than notebooking. As a die-hard notebooking mama, it was difficult to decide to give the kids workbooks even when life required it.

Do you know what? The kids are still thriving! They are

still learning! Even though I can't always teach the way I love to teach, I've had to learn not to be so hard on myself when I can't meet my own expectations.

It is during these times that the Lord shows Himself faithful. He picks up the slack in ways that I could never anticipate, often in unexpected, wonderful ways! In these seasons, I have come to understand more about God's provision and His strength being made perfect in weakness.

Can you relate? By surrendering to seasons, we learn to listen to other things that God might be teaching us during those times. Oh, the grief I could have saved myself by simply changing the expectations I placed on myself instead of pushing so hard and feeling guilty for what I wished we were accomplishing instead of appreciating what God was doing. Oftentimes, I have pushed myself and my kids too hard by simply expecting life to go on as usual, even when the circumstances of life changed.

Over the years, I've learned (mostly the hard way), that I must flex more. The kids do better when I yield to the season of life we are in, but the real winner is me. I am less stressed out and a whole lot more pleasant to be around! Come to think of it, everyone wins and our home is a happier, more peaceful place.

Just About the Time I Figure Things Out...

Whenever I get comfortable with our homeschool and family routine, I know it's about to change. Not long ago, I was schooling two high schoolers. Now, one has graduated and is taking college classes. The second is on the verge of graduating and has a job in town. This means I have a lot less help at home. Just after our oldest daughter graduated, our five-year old entered kindergarten. Another adjustment. More flexibility required.

What season are you in? Ask the Lord to show you how to fit your life to the season your family is in. Be realistic about your circumstances when you are creating your schedule, choosing curriculum, and deciding which activities you wish to do outside your home. You may be in a season where doing activities outside your home will bring more stress than blessing into your life.

POA #1
Seek the Lord for guidance!

The POA here is easy. It should always be the first one on your list anyway: Plan to talk with the Lord. It's worth it to sit back and really ask Him for guidance. And don't forget to talk with your husband, too! Chances are good that he'll have some great insight into your season, since he's sharing it with you!

Blessed are the flexible, for they shall not break.

Flexible Scheduling

In case you haven't noticed, I am a typical "type A" personality. I like to have order to my day. I love a well-planned routine. Routines are good for mamas and they're even better for children!

POA #2
Plan on making a schedule.

Schedules are wonderful. They can bring order to chaos, because with a thoughtful routine in place, everyone knows what they are supposed to be doing at any given time. This is particularly helpful on days when Mom isn't feeling so great.

Every busy homeschool mom I know has some sort of schedule, whether she has it written down or not. God must like routine. He's a God of order, after all! The sun comes up, and goes down ... on a schedule!

HOWEVER.

Schedules were made for the busy homeschool mom, not the other way around. In other words—make your schedule. Color code it. Tape it to the refrigerator. Call a family meeting and explain the schedule.

And then, plan to hold onto it loosely.

Why? Because life will get in the way of your routine, and you've got to be ready to flex when you need to. If you hold loosely to your plan, you'll survive and even thrive when life throws a monkey wrench into your routine. And so will your kids.

POA #2? Plan on making a schedule. More on that in a bit.

Planning Time for Yourself

Every busy homeschool mom needs a break.

Over the years, I have noticed that the last people to take breaks tend to be

POA #3
Make time for yourself.

mothers! There is just too much to do. But neglecting yourself in order to take care of your kids will eventually backfire. Trust me. My kids have seen the smoke!

Homeschooling is a very time-intensive undertaking. It requires moms to stand at the ready most of the daylight hours. It's a constant pouring out of one's self. And that's good! But at the end of the day, you can't keep pouring into the lives of others if you are not being filled up on occasion, too.

I am talking to myself here, as well. I'm not very good at

this. It's very difficult for me to take time to do the most basic things sometimes—like exercise. I usually consider exercise something to do *if I have time* instead of making it a priority. But on the days when I get outside and go for that walk, I feel so much better. It's amazing what a twenty-minute walk will do for my perspective!

The same thing is true in many other areas of life. A dear friend of mine is a great example of knowing when to take a break. I call her "Fun Country Carol" because I know that if I ever need a break, that woman is up for just about anything! She'd drop her routine to go to the park or out for coffee. And she makes other people feel loved because she's got a great balance to homeschool and the rest of life. I want to be like her when I grow up.

So I'll tell you what Carol often tells me: "Taking time for yourself is not optional." The POA here? Go get a haircut. Or take a nap. Read a book that fills you up. Journal about your life. Treat yourself to a bubble bath after the kids are in bed. Light some candles *just because*. Recharge your batteries, busy homeschool mom! You'll be so glad you did … and your kids will too!

White Space

In *The Busy Homeschool Mom's Guide to Romance*, I touched on something I like to call "white space." For those of you who have not read the book, white space has a very simple definition: it is a few days in a row of unscheduled time. The key here is to take them exactly as prescribed—in a row. Can you believe this busy homeschool mom said that? I mean it. White space is essential to successfully navigating the homeschool years.

POA #4
Create some white space.

What do I mean by having nothing on your calendar? Easy! I mean...

Nada. Zero. Zippo. Nothin'.

For some of you, that means you need to PLAN to do nothing. That's right! Give yourself *at least* two days a week *in a row* that don't have anything written down to do. (Hence the term, white space.) This means no doctor appointments, no planned activities, nowhere to go.

Keeping free space on your calendar opens the time up for one of two things:

1. Spontaneity
    -or-
2. Rest

Either way, white space is a winner. For me, it's one of the best-kept secrets of successfully navigating the busy homeschool years.

What does your calendar look like? If you don't have at least two days in a row of white space every week, it's time to make some changes.

CHAPTER 2

Organized Daylight

CONTROLLING CLUTTER AND RECLAIMING YOUR SPACE

*Don't own so much clutter
that you will be relieved to see your house catch fire.*
~ Wendell Berry

One roadblock to developing a POA for your day may easily be your lack of organization. It's difficult to create a successful rhythm to your day if you are surrounded by another set of not-so-wonderful twins I like to call Chaos and Clutter. Left unmanaged, these brats will drain you of your time and energy. They are the nemesis of every busy homeschool mom. Along with their cousin, Excess, they are the enemy of a peaceful, organized home.

Did you know that there is an emotional cost to the things that you own? We live in a culture of excess. Most of the time, we think of clutter as taking physical space but it costs emotionally as well as financially. Clutter and disorganization in our homes can rob us of peace and restfulness at home, leading to feelings of frustration and anxiety. How many of you reading this book have said, "Darling, please go get your math book," only to spend the next two hours turning the house upside down looking for it?

Me too!

It's easy to see how too much clutter and too many piles of unfinished business at home cause us to feel overwhelmed and discouraged with life.

Many moms would rather ignore the mess and try instead to simply work around it, but I promise you that getting a grip on your stuff will translate into more hours in your day! If that sounds appealing to you, then get ready to purge and simplify.

You probably don't need all that stuff you have. And besides ...

You Can't Take it With You

Learning to control physical clutter is an absolutely essential skill if you want to manage your day well. I learned this early on in life from my grandparents.

My grandmother on my father's side was a packrat. Now, don't get me wrong—I loved her dearly. She sewed the most amazing things and she made the best fudge I have ever eaten in my life. The only problem was that it was nearly impossible to find our way to the kitchen to eat it! She literally had to create paths through dozens of boxes and clutter so that we could find our way there.

As much as I loved my grandma, it was stressful to be at her home for too long. Piles of unorganized paperwork, laundry, groceries and garage sale items covered every flat surface in her little apartment. It was frustrating for her, too, because finding her car keys in under an hour was nearly impossible. Grandma had a clutter problem.

Grandma knew that one of the secrets to a quiet, contented household was simple organization.

Grandma Forsberg was the complete opposite. My mother's mother, she was neat almost to a fault (which is why finding a balance is so important)! To Grandma Forsberg, cleanliness was next to godliness. Grandma knew that one of the secrets to a quiet, contented household was simple organization. She had a place for everything—and at the end of the day, everything was in its place.

This attitude was adopted into my mom's household, too, and it helped me tremendously when I became a wife and mother. Mom taught us to keep our rooms clean and to clean up after ourselves as we were growing up. Having a place for everything kept our home neat and tidy, even though there were nine people there most of the time!

Chaos and clutter actually impede our ability to live freely and peacefully, because physical clutter eventually results in mental clutter. There is something deeply satisfying about simplifying life. We can simplify our things, our schedules and our homeschooling. I like to start with physical clutter though, because clearing the clutter at home frees us in so many more ways than just physical space. It brings emotional freedom as well.

Are you ready to simplify and de-clutter your home? Before you can organize, you've got to prioritize. You've got to get rid of excess. We were created by a God of order—so it makes sense that we function better when there is order in our homes.

Clutter's Last Stand

clut·ter/ˈklətər/

Verb: Crowd (something) untidily; fill with clutter.

Noun: A collection of things lying about in an untidy mess.

Have you ever felt stressed out by all the stuff around you? Many families today struggle with clearing the clutter out of their homes. Homeschool moms are no different except that we've got even more things to sort through! Sometimes, it's difficult to know what to keep and what to toss.

Sometimes we keep things for sentimental reasons. Other times, we keep unused items we don't really need just in case we have the opportunity to use them later. I have been guilty of all of these kinds of excuses to keep clutter around at various points in my adult life.

For example, a friend gave me her expensive juicer several years ago. She didn't use it anymore, and thought I might enjoy it since I love to make green smoothies for our kids. Even though I wasn't sure I needed the juicer, I was too afraid to hurt her feelings and turn down such an expensive gift. She brought it over and I put it on our kitchen counter.

That huge juicer sat on my kitchen counter—unused—for about six months. I kept telling myself I would use it but, for whatever reason, I never found the motivation to add that appliance to my daily routine. When I finally accepted that I wasn't going to use it regularly, I moved it to our garage where it collected dust for three years!

We moved that heavy thing from one shelf to the next, trying to make room for even more things we didn't use until one day ... I'd had enough. I snapped. There was so much stuff in my garage that I didn't know where to begin cleaning it up. I didn't even have the emotional or physical energy to hold a garage sale and I ended up giving about $1,500 worth of stuff away on Craigslist to the first ~~sucker~~ person who claimed it. Jay and I stood by the curb and watched as people from all over town came and claimed our things. It was a weird feeling to see things that had been in our home for years leave with strangers but, since I was so ready to part with them, it was easier than I thought it would be. "Buh-bye, stuff! So long, Chaos, Clutter and Excess!"

An Emotional Drain

It was so freeing to see things that we were not using leave in someone else's car! So freeing, in fact, that I began to go through our whole house and get rid of even more things that we no longer used or needed, many of them duplicate items.

The more we purged, the better I felt.

Here's the thing: I had not realized how much emotional energy I was putting in to finding a place for all the things that were constantly coming into our home. Letting go of things I had been hanging onto but did not need or love was freeing. Having less clutter around made our home feel more peaceful and less stressful, even though we lived in a modest-sized house with six children. After the garage was organized, I headed to the kitchen. I got rid of extra can openers, bowls I never used, knives I didn't need, and little gadgets (some of them still in their store packaging). The extra coffee maker I kept "just in case" ours broke and the cookie press that looked cool but I had used only once in 15 years went too. It wasn't all junk, either. Wonderful things we purchased or received as gifts over the years but never got around to using were put into boxes and donated to a local thrift shop.

Voila! More space in the kitchen cupboards meant more space on the kitchen counter tops. Our kitchen felt more spacious and inviting. I found I had room to display beloved photographs and other things that made us smile.

As the children saw me cleaning out kitchen cupboards and cleaning off bookshelves, they began to catch a vision for what I was doing. Pretty soon, they were motivated to clear out their toys, closets and even their dressers! We made dozens of trips to a charity drop off site over the summer as we purged and organized our home.

The result was more room for the kids to run, less stuff to worry about, less stuff to dust (amen!) and more room in my mind to think about other things. (Scary, I know.) It was wonderful.

Now before you think our home is neat and clutter free all the time, or that I was able to do this overnight, let me be very clear: It took us a long time to clear the clutter from our home. To be honest, we still have to keep an eye on it. Just last week I was helping two of our younger daughters (elementary school age) clean their room. I was amazed at how much stuff was lurking under the bed, behind closet doors, and stuffed into dressers. Birthday party favors, stained clothes, unmatched socks. That's just the way it goes.

But if you stay on top of it, it's easier to tame.

Help Your Children Hold Loosely

Moms, you are training your kids in so much more than academics. You're teaching them life skills. As your children see you placing importance in keeping clutter to a minimum and holding loosely to things, they will have a model to take into adulthood as well.

I've tried to create a process for getting rid of things in our house that is easy for the kids to follow. We keep a large plastic bin at the top of the stairs to be filled regularly by every member of our family. Toys that they have outgrown or no longer enjoy, clothes that don't fit or that we simply don't need, extra blankets, lamps, you name it—if we don't need it, it goes in the bin.

When the bin is full, I put those things into a bag and they are donated to a thrift store or given to a friend who I know could use them. The point is, we don't keep things that are in the bin.

Giving these things away is not only good for you, it's good for your kids. It's a skill they will need and use for the rest of their lives!

Defining Clutter

You may be looking around you wondering how to dig out from under the excess and clutter in your home. If so, you're not alone! If you're wondering what defines clutter, allow me to provide you with a brief explanation of how we determine what clutter is in our home. This will help you start to recognize what you can keep and what you need to get rid of.

• **Clutter is anything that is disorganized.**

In our home, everything has a place. That's not to say
everything is always in its place but at the end of the
day, we know where things go. We know it's cluttered
when things have strayed from their home and got
mixed up with everything else. Toys left on the floor.
Mail sitting on the entryway table or kitchen counter.
Shoes in the toy box (it happens all the time) in the
hallway or by the front door. Clothes that need to be
put away. Schoolwork piled up on the kitchen table.
I could go on and on. Essentially, anything that is
disorganized or untidy is clutter.

• **Clutter is anything you don't need or love.**

This is a big one. This is the question I had to ask
when I did my first big cleanup. Training the kids
to ask this question has helped them to define what
they really want to keep as opposed to what they feel
they might want later. It has also helped us to define
what we truly value in life. When a home is filled
with things we love, rather than things we are just
keeping around for a rainy day, it helps us to truly
love where we live.

• **Clutter is too much stuff in too small a space.**
This is often a busy homeschool mom's struggle.
Books that take up too much space on a shelf. A
schoolroom that is so overfilled no one uses it. Too
many papers in a box on the desk. Too many clothes
in one drawer. Too many items on the bathroom
counter or too much furniture in one room. No
matter how creative your storage solutions are—too
many bins are still too many.

Mostly though, clutter is just *too much* stuff. I really
believe it frees us mentally and emotionally when we scale
down. It's amazing how freeing it is to come home to a clean,
uncluttered house at the end of the day, or to wake up to a tidy
kitchen in the morning. I don't know about you, but looking
at clean bookshelves and a tidy school area makes me feel like
I've got a better grip on homeschooling.

Where Do I Start? Use Zones!

People ask us all the time how we keep our house tidy
and neat. Let me just say this right up front: our house is NOT
always neat and tidy. We usually start our days off with a clean

and tidy house but within an hour or two it seriously looks like a bomb has gone off in several areas.

Over the years, I've discovered that the key to living peacefully with a houseful of kids is to have a plan to keep order rather than an expectation that the house should look like a show home from *Better Homes and Gardens* all the time!

We have tried different methods for keeping up with housework during different seasons of life in our family. When all the children were very young, a schedule taped to the refrigerator door helped a lot. On it, we had areas of our home divided into zones. Each child was assigned one of these zones.

A zone might be the hallway and guest bathroom, the entry way or kitchen. Even little ones can have their own zone: our three year old loved tidying her zone ... it was her toy box!

Mornings and afternoons are great times to train the kids to tidy up the house. When Jay was working outside of our home, we tried to have the house neat and welcoming for him when he arrived home from work. There is something really wonderful about coming home to a clean, tidy house and zones really work.

The best thing about zones though, is that you can use them to tidy up for company in no time flat! This is because you're not trying to figure out which parts of the house need attention: everyone just tidies up his or her zone.

DAILY CHORES & ZONES

12th Grader	11th Grader	9th Grader	5th Grader	3rd Grader	1st Grader
Your zone is what you check before you go to bed each night. Please keep it clean, it's your responsibility.					
Zone 1	**Zone 2**	**Zone 3**	**Zone 4**	**Zone 5**	**Zone 6**
Up Bath.	Family Rm.	Garage	Trashman!	Entry Way	Coat Closet
Living Rm.	Guest Bath	Recycling	TV Room	School Room	Toybox
Up Hall	Office	Stairs		Laundry	Bedroom
Bedroom	Bedroom	Bedroom		Bedroom	
M-Breakfast	M-Laundry	M-Vacuum	M-Vacuum	M-Dinner	M-Breakfast
T-Dinner	T-Breakfast	T-Garbage	T-Dinner	T-Laundry	T-Dinner
W-Tutor Day	W-Vacuum	W-Laundry	W-Breakfast	W-Kitchen	W-Toilets
Th-Vacuum	Th-Dinner	Th-Breakfast	Th-Laundry	Th-Dust FR	Th-Mirrors
F-Laundry	F-Dust LR	F-Dinner	F-Dust LR	F-Breakfast	F-Laundry

Breakfast is helping grandma.
Dinner means you help with dinner cleanup and prep.
Laundry means running laundry through. Every person folds and puts away their own clothes. If it's your day, that includes the baby's clothes.

Each Morning:	Do what is listed for that day after you've had breakfast and gotten schoolwork out.
Every Afternoon:	Quick zone check.
Every Evening:	Finish your day's chore and check your zone.

One Thing at A Time

When your home is filled with clutter, trying to tackle a mountain of stuff can be quite overwhelming. It's easy to get discouraged by a task that seems insurmountable when you're trying to raise a family and homeschool at the same time!

So here's my advice: start with just fifteen minutes at

a time. You can do just about anything in fifteen minutes a day! Here are some great ways to get started, fifteen minutes at a time.

Create a place for incoming papers. I'm not just talking about mail, either. I'm talking about all paper that you need to sort. Receipts, prescriptions, schoolwork, letters. If it's junk mail, don't keep it another second. Toss it. This one simple step will save you hours of time organizing and will make a huge difference in simplifying your space.

Clear off a counter. It's amazing to me how quickly flat surfaces in our home fill up. Car keys, purses, bills, dishes, books, you name it. Eventually though, you want to get these clutter keeping spaces cleared out. Start with one counter. Clear off everything possible, leaving only the essentials. Put away everything you don't use all the time.

Take fifteen things out of your house...for good. Take a bag and start filling it. Most of us can quickly go into a bathroom, a closet or the kitchen and find fifteen things we no longer use or enjoy. As soon as you have a minimum of fifteen things, take them out to your car. Keep them there so that when you're in town running errands, you can drop them off at a charity site.

- Tidy one small area. It can be the entry-way, guest bathroom or dining room. Spend five minutes focused just on that one area.

- Clean out your medicine cabinet. I did this a few years ago. To my amazement, I had medicine in there from when I was still single! Throw it out, Mom! Go through your cabinet and search for everything non-essential. Bandaids that look like they won't stick, old makeup, ointments that you have used once in five years—it all needs to go.

- Write down what rooms need your attention first. If you can write them all down in order of priority, you can come up with a game plan to tackle the job.

Once you have written down which rooms need the most attention, choose one to start in. Just getting one room done will motivate you toward success and spur you on to your next room. It's a lot like being on a diet! Losing two pounds is good motivation to continue on and lose two more.

Start small. One step at a time! I'm going to start with a plan for organizing larger rooms. If you don't have a designated schoolroom, that's okay. You can use this as a template for many areas in your home: living or family room, dining room, bedroom. The method for organizing it is still the same.

Organizing Large Rooms

Here's the best way I have found to tackle larger rooms. As I thought about what works for keeping our busy house fairly organized, I realized that I can boil it down to five basic steps. Don't you love that? Keep it simple, busy homeschool mom!

If you have older children, train them to work alongside you and encourage them to offer their suggestions as you rearrange and organize. Some of our kids are really gifted in this area, and allowing them in on the process has not only trained them, it has been a huge blessing to me!

1. Before you start, set out four containers, either boxes or bags. One is for items you will keep, one for giveaway (whether you garage sale, donate, or whatever), one is for items you are not sure what to do with, and one is for trash.

2. Empty the room. I know this sounds crazy but if things have gotten out of hand, it's the best way to start. Empty the room as much as you possibly can—right down to the bookshelves. Empty them, too. Come to think of it, since the room is being emptied, it is a good time to rearrange the furniture if you like to do that sort of thing.

3. If your husband or older children are around, make it a family project. After all, it didn't get cluttered up by itself, and training your kids to part with clutter will help them tremendously later in life. Make sure everyone knows that the goal is to simplify, simplify, simplify! It's hard work, but it's worth it. When I am getting ready to organize things, I expect things to get worse before they get better, and I warn the family ahead of time—it could take a few days before we are finished.

4. Sort as you go. As you empty the room, start sorting. BE BRUTAL about what you decide to keep. Ask yourself, "Do I love this?" and if you don't answer yes immediately, it's time to get rid of it, or set it into a separate box to get back to. When

sorting curriculum, you may decide to store things for later use or set them aside for a used curriculum sale, *eBay*, etc. If that's the case, you still need to get that stuff out of the room. I like to have boxes ready to label for this purpose.

5.   Be sure that as you put things into boxes you clearly label them so there is no guessing as to what is inside. I also set a box of curriculum aside to give to other homeschool moms. I might take it to our homeschool co-op or call a few moms to see if they are interested in going through it and taking what they would like.

6.   Say goodbye. When the room is empty and everything has been sorted, it's time to take the giveaway/throwaway things out of your house.

7.   Don't look back. Put them in your car.

8.   I have a rule at home that when it goes in the giveaway bag, no one can sort through it and take things back out, because if we really needed it or loved it, it wouldn't be in the bag in the first place. Also, feel free to talk to your junk as you take it out to your car. Buh-bye, clutter! Good-

bye, pencil sharpener that I never liked and lamp that we never use. See ya, books that no one reads! Au revoir, scrapbook supplies from 1995 and the guilt that came with not using them! Nighty-night, picture frames that we never hung! Are you getting a good visual of what it looks like to declutter? I hope so! It really is freeing when you begin to let go of things—because then your things don't have a hold on you anymore.

9. Keep sorting, and take a deep breath, busy homeschool mom, 'cause you're going to feel a whole lot better when this is done!

10. Move Back In. Once you have taken all the giveaway and trash items out of your house, it's time for the really fun part—moving things back into the space you cleared out. I am a big fan of keeping beautiful baskets on shelves for organizing. We have baskets with scrap paper in them and baskets that are full of colored pencils. I believe that we even have a basket for storing extra baskets! Point is, EVERYTHING has a place. When you bring things back into the room, have a vision for how you want to display

what you keep. For an item to come back in the room, it should:

❖ Fit neatly into a designated space.

❖ Be something you truly love or use regularly.

❖ Not exceed a reasonable number of items. In other words, do you *really* need 200 pencils on the shelf? Probably not. Find a place for the extra pencils that is out of sight but easy to get to.

Creative Storage Ideas

Finding creative storage solutions is so easy these days! I love finding new ways to organize because it allows me to be creative and change with the landscape of our family. Being a mom of seven, I have had ample opportunity to try out many methods of organization over the years. Most of them work. When you look to organize your schoolroom, keep in mind that if you love the look, you will be more likely to keep it neat and tidy long term.

Keep your eyes open for creative containers to store things in. I have found some of my favorite containers at garage sales! When you are at second-hand stores, look for pretty baskets that will hide some of the more "necessary" clutter, like scrap paper and art supplies. We have a shelf in our schoolroom that has four clear plastic containers neatly lined up together for crayons, colored pencils, erasers, and regular pencils. The best part about the clear plastic is that even little ones who cannot read can see where these things are supposed to go.

One more little note about containers: I forgo lids whenever possible. We lose them anyway. If I am storing away something that will not be used often, it has a lid. If I am simply trying to organize something on a shelf (like pencils or crayons), it does not.

Keeping School Records

Transcripts. Standardized tests. "Record of work done". These words have struck fear into the heart of many a homeschool mom. The idea of keeping meticulous track of school assignments is daunting for a mom with one child, let alone four or more! As a new homeschooler, the idea of record keeping overwhelmed me. I did the best I could, storing the kids' work in file folders

Make sure your children are in the habit of writing their name and the date on their schoolwork!

and dating worksheets so that I knew when we finished them, but my methods weren't exactly user-friendly and it certainly was not something I was excited about doing.

Like it or not, though, you need to keep records of your child's schoolwork. Clunky record keeping is not what you want.

In our home, we do quite a bit of notebooking, along with workbooks for math and (in the early years) phonics. The notebooks have become each child's record of written work—and we love them! But I will admit, making sure the right papers ended up in the right notebooks every day was challenging and frustrating at times.

So I simplified. Are you starting to see a pattern?

Today, we use a very simple method for keeping track of school papers and notebooking assignments. Instead of having the kids put their papers in the appropriate notebook at the end of the day, ALL of their assignments, love notes, darling drawings that I can't part with and artwork go in one box.

That's it! Each day, as the children finish their work, they know that they are supposed to write their name and date on the assignment and then put it in the "completed assignments" box. This keeps my table clear of clutter and my mind free from worrying about losing their work.

About once a quarter, we empty the box, saving their best work in sheet protectors and putting them in their notebooks in chronological order. Each child has a notebook. We throw away things that we don't love or need to keep. That's it! Simple and effective.

Organizing School Books

This is a great topic because there are a gazillion ways to do it and every family is different. The trick to organizing your school space is to keep it simple and do what works best for the season of life you're in.

For example, if you are on bed rest, you might want to store workbooks and other homeschooling supplies by the couch. If you are moving, keep them in a portable container. Even a backpack will do.

At our home, we have one bookshelf with dedicated homeschool space on it. All the younger kids know that they are to return their things to their shelf at the end of each day. That way, I can find school books when I need to, and we spend a lot less time searching for things at the beginning of each school day.

We keep our pens and pencils on a windowsill next to

the pencil sharpener—all within easy reach of the kitchen table, where we do most of our homeschooling. Again, keep things simple.

Laundry (Mount Never-rest) Ideas

Ahhh, the laundry room. I love my laundry room. In it, sit two of the best inventions of the 21st century: a washing machine and a dryer. And sometimes, a laptop computer! Yes, I have been known to write in my laundry room. The smell of clean laundry is comforting to me and I love the humming sound that the washing machine makes. It's the sound of productivity!

I love the sense of accomplishment that folding laundry brings me. There is just something about pulling clothes out of the dryer and folding them that makes me happy. It's probably a sickness but I've decided to go with "it works for me" when it comes to tackling this big job. I've tried almost every laundry solution I have heard about over the years, too.

After twenty-two years of marriage and seven children, I think I may have found a solution that works better than any of the others. Adopting this new method involved two main things:

❖ Surrendering my desire to have every item folded perfectly

❖ Willingness to let my children go without clean clothes if they failed to do their own laundry.

Notice it has nothing to do with a method. *It's all about my attitude*. Yep! You guessed it! I don't do laundry much anymore, even though I really do enjoy it. I simply have too many other things that truly need my attention.

Put Your Kids To Work!

Yes, that's right. Even little ones can learn to operate your washer and dryer! I know, because at our house, our kids do it. Even the five year old is in on the laundry action, with a little routine that is all hers.

Some of you are way ahead of me on this and you're probably saying, "DUH!!" right now, but for those of you who are still holding on to your perfectly folded towels and neatly pressed shirts, let me just tell you that releasing this chore to the kids was one of the best homemaking decisions I ever made.

Here's how we do it. Instead of each person in our family

THE BUSY HOMESCHOOL MOM'S GUIDE

doing his or her own laundry, we divide the task by rooms. This allows those who are share a bedroom to work together on laundry. It also cuts down on the number of loads being done, and has the added side benefit of helping prepare the kids for life on their own.

Five Steps for Saving Time in the Laundry Room

Sort by room, not by person. Each bedroom has its own laundry hamper and its own laundry basket. Sharpie markers are used to write the bedroom name (i.e. little boys' room) on each hamper. Hampers stay in the bedrooms until they are full and need to be washed.

Each room has a basket that sits on the counter in the laundry room. As the laundry comes out of the dryer, it is put into the appropriate basket. Sometimes, a child will start their laundry and then not be home to run it through. This is when having their own basket in the laundry room comes in very handy. It's easy for another child to take their clothes out of the dryer and put them into the correct basket without much effort.

🕐 You wear it, you wash it. The children are responsible for running their own clothes through as well as folding and putting their own laundry away. If they go into the laundry room and there are clothes in the washer or dryer, they move them through the cycle.

🕐 Each child, down to the five year old, can run both machines. It's much easier now that we use front loaders, but when we had top loaders, we had a little stool next to the washer for the shorter laundry doers. This took a little training (and a few ruined articles of clothing), but it was worth it for the freedom that came from allowing the children to serve in this way.

🕐 Keep it moving. I have a friend who charges her kids hard cash if their clothes aren't in their drawer the same day they're laundered. So far, I haven't had to do that because the sheer amount of laundry that's done at our house doesn't leave much time for lolly-gagging laundry goers! There is always someone next in line so the laundry moves through fairly quickly. Since all the kids know the drill, they move the laundry along as necessary.

🕐 Community property is community responsibility.

Anything that comes into the laundry room that's not the property of an individual, such as towels and table cloths, is washed and folded by the person who is next in line to wash clothes. Kitchen towels are taken to the laundry room by the children who are cleaning the kitchen, and so on.

Backup Happens. Life is never predictable. As much as I would like to say that we have a perfect system and that things are always done according to plan, they're not. Occasionally I find myself with a laundry room full of clean clothes that need to be folded and put away. When this happens, a family folding party is usually the remedy. Be creative. Stay flexible. Keep trying new things!

Socks are still my nemesis and are usually put into the sock basket if they are not matched immediately out of the dryer. About once a year, I contemplate moving to Arizona, just so we can spend more time in flip flops than we do wearing socks. Who knows. We may do that yet... and if we do, you'll know why!

An Organized Office = Less Stressful Daylight

We are privileged to share a home out in the beautiful Washington countryside with Jay's mom and dad. Jay's mom, Jerry, is an expert organizer and so we have had fun trying new ways to keep our shared office neat and tidy. A few months ago, Jerry and I took on the task of re-organizing our office. It had been a year since we had done it—and believe me, it showed!

The kids helped us take everything out except for the big desk, right down to extra chairs and shelves. I wish I had kept pictures of the process because it was something to see. We managed to fill six huge bags with items to give away. It's amazing how fast we accumulate things!

I always recommend taking everything out of the room you are working on and then putting things back in as you purge and sort. However, if you don't have time to do that, start with the one area of your office that is the primary feature: your desk.

Clear off the desk top first. Throw anything away that you don't need or that is garbage. Remember to be tough on yourself as you purge. Haven't used it in a few months? Store it in a box in the garage and then, if you haven't used it in six months, consider getting rid of it, too. Keep that garbage can handy!

File important papers. We have a filing system in our house that I love. Every utility bill has its own file, and other things are easily categorized. For example, under "School," I have three sub-folders: HSLDA membership info, WA state homeschool law, and annual testing information. The children have individual folders as necessary but this way, I know where to find important information in a hurry.

Sort mail as soon as it arrives at your house. Mail, be it junk or otherwise, comes every day and can easily get out of control if you don't have a POA for it. Have a box or a bin where you can easily put your incoming mail.

Clean out desk drawers. Just like you would clean out a room—empty those drawers completely. I usually dump the drawer into a cardboard box and then begin putting things back while separating junk from necessary items.

Wipe the desk drawers out and put things back that you truly need. How often do you send out Easter cards, anyway? If you don't use them all the time, they don't belong in your desk. Put them away with seasonal things if necessary, and store them where you can find them when you need them.

Make Daily Cleanup a Habit

Have you ever learned to play an instrument or participated in a sport? If you have, then you know how important practice and consistency is if you want to learn a new skill!

Keeping your home free of clutter is a skill. Practice keeping up with it in the same way you would practice to learn any other skill. Once you are organized, it's not going to require much effort to keep things that way. Get into the habit of putting things where they go as soon as you are through using them.

Here are some more quick tips for making sure your new, organized self stays that way:

❖ Create a space for everything from car keys to tennis shoes.

❖ When something new comes in, consider letting something else go.

❖ Make sure the kids are responsible for tidying up their zones.

❖ Practice hospitality—celebrate by inviting company over for dinner or hosting an event at your house. There's nothing like company to motivate your inner cleanup girl!

Can't you just feel a more organized daylight coming? Life is made much easier when you don't have to waste precious time hunting for something that's been misplaced because of clutter.

And remember, organizing your daylight hours is all about managing your time. Carve out some time in your daily routine for cleanup and organizing. You'll be glad you did!

CHAPTER 3

Scheduled Daylight

THE DELIGHT AND THE DANGERS
OF SCHEDULING

*I am definitely going to take a course
on time management…
just as soon as I can work it into my schedule.*
~ Louis E. Boone

WARNING! This chapter is meant to be an encouragement, not a template. If you have trouble seeing other people's schedules without feeling guilty about your own, skip this chapter and go directly to the LAST chapter of this book before reading this one. It's called *Surrendered Daylight: Finding HIS Heart for Your Homeschool.*

All moms face the challenge of how to prioritize their time. Time management becomes absolutely critical, though, for moms who have taken on the specialized demands of homeschooling. Homeschool moms devote an average of six hours each day to the task of homeschooling. Because of this, it's crucial to streamline and simplify as much as possible during the homeschool years.

Each day, we're given the chance to spend the gift of time as we see fit. Some days, we spend it better than others and joyfully announce the list of things we accomplished that day on Facebook. Other times, we waste the time we have been given and it leaves us feeling defeated and frustrated at the end of the day.

We are stewards of our own time. We can blame it on whatever we want to (and I realize that some things truly are out of our control), but for the most part, we are the ones responsible for how we choose to manage our time.

At our home, we are productive most days because, like most busy moms, I've learned the hard lessons of poor time management. I've wallowed in my lack of self-control (because that's really what it is) and I've blamed everyone but myself for it from time to time.

Having an "off" day is one thing, but when poor time management becomes the rule rather than the exception, it's time to get things back into focus and set some goals for managing the daylight hours more effectively. I like to start by making a list (Surprise, surprise!) of what I value most in my day.

Time is at a premium for most families with children at home. But for homeschool moms, it's even more essential that we learn to manage our time well in order to make the most of the homeschool years.

Prioritizing Your Day

Years ago, I came up with three priorities to help me decide where I would invest the time I had each day. Today, I think of it as a sort of guideline for determining how I will prioritize the time God gives me. Every day, I strive to make time for these things:

I CHOOSE...

- ❖ To spend time in God's Word each day.
- ❖ To spend time alone with my husband each day.
- ❖ To be intentional about managing our home by looking at each day with specific goals in mind to accomplish. This means that I schedule our days.

Yep! I know it sounds boring and stuffy to some of you,

but scheduling has saved my bacon on more than one occasion. On days when I feel too tired to think straight, out comes the schedule and the kids know exactly what they are supposed to be doing without me telling them over and over ... and over.

On other days, we might have time and energy for some spontaneous unscheduling and I'll ditch the schedule altogether in favor of reading longer with the children or catching my husband for an impromptu lunch date. Either way, that schedule is there to help keep us moving in the direction we want to go.

Maybe it's some sort of neurosis, but I've discovered that having a system or schedule in place allows my mind to let go of things that would otherwise drive me completely out onto a limb such as handwriting practice and memory work. If I have it in a schedule, I know it is going to get done.

Here's the key to successful scheduling though: there's not one right way to do it. You've got to give yourself freedom to try new things.

Different Strokes for Different Folks

Your schedule should be as unique as your homeschool— and since there are many, many different ways to create a schedule for your family, I thought I'd collect a few and show them to you for comparison.

Think of these schedules as opportunities for you to glean from what is working for others, not a mandate for what you should be doing. As you look at different schedules, take what is appealing to you and highlight it! It might be just the thing you need to jumpstart your own daily routine. You will notice that some schedules are very light while others are very detailed and down-to-the-minute.

What about Academics?

Most families find that it's easier to concentrate on academics in the morning when minds are fresh and moms aren't frazzled. Children are usually at their best in the mornings, too. Afternoons can be spent in playtime for the younger ones and independent study for the older ones.

Many books I've read prescribe a particular method for scheduling schoolwork but, from my experience, most moms are not "typical."

That's the beauty of homeschooling! You can fit it to meet the needs of your own family in order to get the most out of your days.

I Felt So Much Better After That!

When I was a brand-new homeschool mom, I simply could not find enough practical, detailed information about how other people homeschooled. As we approached year three of our homeschool adventure, I found a book by Diana Waring called "Things We Wished We'd Known." I bought that book and practically devoured it. Hearing the real life experiences of other moms gave me renewed perspective. I felt so much better after that!

After all, the home is the domain of the woman. She sets the tone at home, by God's design. If mama's wasting daylight, chances are, everyone else will follow suit.

There is a freedom that comes with finding your own way while you learn from the experience of others! In the pages that follow, you will see a few schedules from other busy homeschool moms. Notice how each one is different. It takes time to find your own rhythm—and it's essential to thriving during the homeschool years. Are you ready to see how different we all are? Here we go!

Sample Schedules and Charts

Daylight Schedules from REAL moms

"EARLY RISERS"

From: Juliet B.

Number of children: 4

Years homeschooling: 8

Juliet says: *Because the kids are all so close in age, we do A LOT of all-together-unit-studies. Technically, they are in 4th, 6th and 7th grades.*

I put our bedtime info on the schedule. We try to get people to brush teeth and put on p.j.s at 8. Then I read aloud. Dad prays about 8:45 and we tuck them in. They read/write/ listen to the radio in bed, but with Dad getting up so early, it's important for us that the house is quiet after 9.

(Dad leaves for work around 5:30 a.m.)

~ Heidi's Notes ~

6:15! I love this mom! She is a MORNING person. I want to be like her when I grow up. She also gives herself permission to have jammie days. When was the last time I did that? Oh yeah. Yesterday. But don't tell anyone. It will be our little secret.

Time	Activity
6:15 a.m.	Mom up. Bible reading.
6:30 a.m.	13 year old twins up—they go straight to the computer to work on their math.
6:45 a.m.	Mom wakes 11 year old up and he showers. Mom may or may not exercise.
7:00 a.m.	Twins do some reading or work on their independent study projects.
7:30 a.m.	Try to make sure the youngest (9) is up. She likes to cuddle with mom in bed for a while to start her day.
8:00 a.m.	Think about breakfast—hopefully kids unload dishwasher.
8:30/ 9:00 a.m.	Start our all-together time: read a chapter from our current read-aloud, do our family bible reading, memory verse work.
Break	Make sure everyone's teeth are brushed, someone may decide to take shower, make bed, get dressed (not everyone gets dressed every day--jammie days are huge around here).
10:00 a.m.	Begin Unit study work all together (this usually covers read aloud, more Bible, history, language arts).
11:15 a.m.	Dad calls home, kids start thinking about lunch. Mom asks them to do their chore wheel chore first

Then lunch, at noon, & sometimes cook together, unless we go to our HS center.

| 12:30 p.m. | Science |

After science: twins finish up reading or independent study work and mom supervises the 2 younger kids with their math

"GO WITH THE FLOW-ERS"

From: Andrea W.

Number of children: 3   Ages: 1, 5 and 7

Years homeschooling: 3

Andrea says: My kids are still little so it's pretty laid back but this is a typical day in our house!

~ Heidi's Notes ~

Andrea's schedule reflects where she is in life right now— she is in a season of having little ones around her. Lots of time for interaction and play with the young ones will set the tone for a great homeschool experience in the coming years.

I also love the 7:00 p.m. bedtime for the baby. At our house, bedtime for younger kids is fairly early, too. Why? Because mama needs to recharge her batteries! It also helps to have a great bedtime routine. Kids tend to thrive on routine, and the bedtime routine is a big one.

Time	Activity
7:00 a.m.	Toddler wakes mama up and 2 older sisters wake up soon after
7:30 a.m.	Morning Routine (get dressed, brush hair, teeth, potty, make bed)
8:00 a.m.	Breakfast/Clean-up
8:30-10:00 a.m.	Free Play which typically involves lots of imagination/creative play, jump rope, dancing.
10:00 a.m.	Snack time
10:30 a.m.	Baby goes down for a nap. Preschool Circle Time with 5 year old.
11:00-12:00 p.m.	School time with my 1st grader (bible devotional, math, reading,writing, spelling, geography 1x week).
12:00-12:30 p.m.	Prep lunch/lunch time.
1:00 p.m.	If it's Thursday, head out the door to take the oldest to sewing lessons (wake baby up if she isn't awake yet) or if not Thursday, free play, puzzles, crafts, doing a playdate, park, etc...
3:30 p.m.	If it's Tuesday, heading out the door for middle daughter's ballet lesson. Otherwise, same as above with free play, reading books with girls, tea party, puzzles, etc...
5:00 p.m.	Preparing dinner
5:30 p.m.	Dinner
7:00 p.m.	Baby in bed
7:30 p.m.	Older 2 bedtime routine, read stories, pray, talk

"WORK AS WE GO'ERS ... WITH TIME TO REST"

From: Angie A.

Number of children: 4   Ages: 8, 6, 4, 2

Years homeschooling: 4

~ Heidi's Notes ~

Angie has a simiplicty to her schedule, and includes working on chores as she goes throughout her day. I am a huge fan of keeping up with the house as our day moves along—but that's not what I love most about Angie's schedule.

Of all the schedules that I have looked at in preparing to write this book, this one really resonated with me for this reason: I love it that Angie has a built-in presure valve written into her daily routine: rest.

This is a challenging thing to pull off—because my natural tendency is to get as much done as I can when the kids are napping or having quiet time. I file papers and make phone calls, finish emails and surf the Internet. I rarely rest. The down side to this approach of course, is the unavoidable mommy burnout.

Good job, Angie, for showing us that rest is important enough to put right on the schedule!

Time	Activity
8:00-9:00 a.m.	Kids: Waking up and morning chores (my husband leaves at about 8:30 a.m.) Morning chores include: Cleaning room, making bed and one child (my Dining room person) gets the laundry upstairs (I have a reverse floor plan, so this helps a lot!) Mom: Starts breakfast/sees husband off/email or other things that are pending.
9:00 a.m.	Kids: (Dining room) sets table and we sit and eat
9:30 a.m.	Upstairs chores before school...(Kitchen: Clears plates to kitchen and helps load/unload dishes/sweeps floor...Dining Room: Wipes table and sweeps floor...Family Room: Pickup/dust/vacuum if needed)
10:00 a.m.	Devotional time: Prayer/worship/daily devotional and discussion
10:30 a.m.	Any other subjects...workbooks, projects, reading, writing, history, science experiments (we are going through a great creation curriculum) and computer learning time after all other work is done.
12:15 p.m.	Kids lunch (working together to get it all out and eaten!)
1:00 p.m.	Mom lunch/kid rest time. I make and eat my lunch, relax, computer time, and time with the Lord. Younger two take naps while older two have quiet time with things to do alone. I do not know what I would do without this time! I am sooo grateful to be able to refresh after teaching and doing so much throughout the day.
3:00 p.m.	Finish up whatever was being worked on/time to play and play games/mom starts dinner and husband comes home...

"PIANO TEACHING MAMA"

From: Jada S.

Number of children: 2   Ages: 8, 6

Years homeschooling: 3

Jada says: I also teach piano lessons to supplement our income. While I am teaching, the kids are with my husband downstairs. Often, he does the read-a-louds with them. They might go play outside or help get dinner ready.

Time	Activity
6:30 a.m.	Wake-up, make bed, get coffee and breakfast ready. Usually, we have easy breakfasts. Get dressed.
7:00 a.m.	Preparing for the day: check email for work. Do any work projects that can be done in the next hour or so.
8:00 a.m.	Begin home schooling the kids before lessons begin. Usually, we begin with Bible. Then, I have the kids do individual subjects as well as art. Group Subjects: Bible, Art, Music, American History, Science, Grammar/Writing Individual: Math, Spelling, Reading (son) and Phonics/Reading (daughter).
8:30 a.m.	Home School
9:00 a.m.	TEACH Piano/voice Lessons (These morning lessons are children of our neighbors, another home schooling family. So, my kids get "social" time with friends while one of the three students are in a piano lesson with me.)

Time	Activity
11:00 a.m.	Lunch
11:30 a.m.	Read-a-louds, American History or Science (we do A.H. 3 days/week and Science 2 days/week)
12:00 p.m.	Continue above OR (See below)
12:30 p.m.	Kids play outside, watch an educational video or have room time and read/play quietly. During this time I get some work done.
1:00 p.m.	Teach Voice Lesson.
1:30 p.m.	Grab a cup of coffee :-)
2:00 p.m.	Finish up any schooling. If complete, kids play, read, arts n' crafts, practice piano, etc. Usually, I get dinner going. If I haven't already (I menu plan weekly, sometimes monthly).
2:30 p.m.	Prepare for afternoon lessons. Husband is usually home. He works from home the remainder of the day, while I teach lessons.
3:00 p.m.	Teach piano and voice
7:00 p.m.	Family Time
7:30 p.m.	Kids get ready for bed.
8:00 p.m.	Kids in bed, prayers, and then...
8:30 p.m.	Mom and Dad time. Usually we are finishing up work for church too.
9:00 p.m.	Relax and watch TV or read.
10:00 p.m.	Lights Out...we have found consistently going to bed at the same time helps us to be more productive during the day as well as in better moods.

"DOWN TO THE MINUTE"

From: Gina W

Number of children: 6

Ages: 8, 6

Years homeschooling: 7

~ Heidi's Notes ~

This is a SCHEDULER. Love how she rotates times with the baby. She knows she needs help and schedules it right in there.

Time	Activity
6:00 a.m.	Get up, read, exercise and shower.
7:00 a.m.	Wake routine for kids (get up, dress, make bed, clean room before breakfast).
7:30 a.m.	Breakfast for all and clean up for all
8:30 a.m.	School begins — Morning routine for all kids (math facts, comprehension page, phonogram drills, etc.)
9:00 a.m.	Math for school age kids (Two toddlers watch Little Bear for 1 hour)
9:30 a.m.	Grammar for school age kids
10:00 a.m.	Break

Time	Activity
10:15 a.m.	Computer lab for two, spelling for two and penmanship for one. One on baby duty.
10:45 a.m.	Rotate subjects and baby duty.
11:15 a.m.	Three are reading, math for one and one gets baby duty.
12:15 p.m.	Lunch for all and clean up for all
1:00 p.m.	Composition, reading, science and one on baby duty.
1:30 p.m.	Nap for mom and baby, all other kids have quiet time and work on undone school work.
2:30 p.m.	Free time for all
3:00 p.m.	Mom does laundry (wash & dry)
4:30 p.m.	Chore time for kids (clean assigned rooms and fold two loads and put away).
5:00 p.m.	Mom gets dinner ready
5:30 p.m.	Dinner for all and clean up for all
6:30 p.m.	History reading/activity for all
7:00 p.m.	Kids read on their beds
8:00 p.m.	Bedtime for kids
8:30 p.m.	Mom does bookkeeping
9:00 p.m.	Hubby time
10:30 p.m.	Bed time for mom

* Alternate schedule for Tuesday & Thursday ~ leave for Karate (all kids) 5:00pm—6:30pm

** Baby duty: puzzles, snack, playdough, draw, blocks, game, outside play, coloring, other activities.

But how do YOU do it?

I knew you were going to ask that sooner or later! I always hesitate to tell people our schedule because inevitably, one of my kids will pipe up and say, "No you don't!! You made that chart but we *neeever* use it!" Usually someone will ask me about our schedule when I am taking a break from it or when I've swapped zones with the kids and decided to change the chart around. It never fails. But that doesn't keep me from pressing onward!

sigh

Schedules should be fluid things. They should bend and flex to make your life easier, not more complicated.

Real life. That's what it is. It's why I tell people that schedules work best when you can flex with the rest of life.

Now that you know how I *really* am, I'll share our family schedule with you. And let me say again: blessed are the flexible! Schedules should be fluid things. They should bend and flex to make your life easier, not more complicated.

Each year it changes a bit, too. In the interest of saving my children from scrutiny I am going to share a schedule from a few years ago. Our current schedule looks a little different because we have a college-age daughter and another who is almost ready to graduate. Each year, things change!

Time	11th gr.	8th gr.	4th gr.	2nd gr.	Kinder.
7:00 a.m.	Rise and shine. Shower, make beds, straighten rooms.				
7:30 a.m.	Breakfast and family devotions.				
8:00 a.m.	Morning chores and zone check.				
8:30 a.m.	Math (dad)	Math (dad)	Math (dad)	Math (grandma)	Reading (mom)
9:30 a.m.	Writing language arts	Writing language arts	Writing language arts	Language Handwriting	Craft
10:30 a.m.	World History and Geography				Read w/ 2nd grader
11:30 a.m.	Chemistry	Astronomy	Astronomy	Astronomy	
12:00 p.m.	Chemistry	Notebooking	Notebooking	Notebooking	
12:30 p.m.	Lunch				
1:00 p.m.	Philosophy	Notebooking and unfinished work			
2:00 p.m.	Wednesdays Music with Dad				

I laugh when I look at this schedule now. Do you know why? Because this one absolutely WILL NOT WORK for me right now. This was a the schedule from two years ago. Since that time, I have had a baby and written another book. Life changes.

This year, we are using checklists and the structured time is much more fluid. Our high school senior studies primarily on her own, with the help of a wonderful lady who tutors her in her final year of science and math.

I've created a detailed checklist for each child this year. You can see a section of one below. This year, the checklist IS the schedule. It's simple. And it's working for this season!

5th Grader - Week Of: November 14 - 18

Weekly assignments in each subject are due by Thursday night.

Science: Astronomy Lesson 13 Stars and Galaxies
- ☐ Read together: pages 147--149 "Light Years" 150-153 "Gospel in the Stars?"
- ☐ 154-158, end of Lesson 13
- ☐ Create a Constellation Planetarium, Page 158, take pictures for your notebook.
- ☐ Arithmetic 5
- ☐ Lesson 29 + speed drill Roman Numerals
- ☐ Lesson 30 + speed drill
- ☐ Lesson 31
- ☐ Lesson 32 is TEST 3

Language/Read & Think 6
- ☐ Reading Comprehension 15

Nothing Good Is Ever Easy

Busy homeschool mom, the day you and your husband decided to homeschool your children, a huge decision was made with regard to how the bulk of your family time would be spent. Teaching your children at home truly is a full-time job.

Because you've chosen homeschooling, you have chosen to let other things go for a certain season of your life. My schedule looks decidedly different from my friends who work outside the home or whose children attend school away from home.

In all honesty, sometimes I'm envious of what appears at least on the outside to be "free time." But no time is truly free. The truth is, we are just exchanging one use of time for another. As homeschool moms, the bulk of our time commitment is spent directly with our children at home rather than running back and forth to events and school.

I know I just confessed to being envious of my friends who don't homeschool from time to time, but I also know that the grass is not greener on the other side! I remember what it was like when my oldest daughter was in school. Life was busy then too—except I was

> Because you have chosen homeschooling, you have chosen to let other things go for a season of your life.

going back and forth to the school building, making time for bake sales and PTA meetings, going on field trips and packing lunches every morning by 7:00 a.m.

I also clearly remember the day I realized that someone besides me was having a *huge influence* on our daughter five days a week, eight hours a day. This realization challenged us to make a life altering decision with regard to how we spent our time.

When we chose to bring Savannah home, we chose to invest our time differently. Now that she is thriving in college, all that scheduling, all the tears, all the laughter, the lessons, the joy, the learning, the growing and even the struggles have yielded much more fruit than we ever imagined. It was worth it. It is worth it. Nothing good is ever easy.

Time passes so quickly, doesn't it? The investment you're making right now in your children is worth it. I'll say it again: It's worth it. When you look at your schedule as a tool to help you spend and invest your time wisely, the challenge can become an opportunity rather than a drudgery.

Scheduling will help you take advantage of every opportunity God gives you as you train up your children. You'll be glad you did, busy homeschool mom! Stay the course.

Nothing worth doing is ever easy. And this thing we call homeschooling, *this* is worth it.

CHAPTER 4

Hungry Daylight

FEEDING YOUR FAMILY
WITHOUT LOSING YOUR MIND

The most remarkable thing about my mother is that for
thirty years she served the family nothing but leftovers.
The original meal has never been found.
~ Calvin Trillin

I love watching cooking shows on TV. It makes me happy. I have passed this love on to a few of our children, too. Most of them will happily watch Emeril with me as he prepares a fish on Thursday afternoon while we fold laundry together. We have passed many delightful afternoons away watching Emeril and sorting socks.

One particular afternoon, just about the time I was beginning to imagine the smell the spices and the taste of the fish that Emeril was cooking, I remembered. It was Thursday. No less than ten people (or more, depending on whether or not the college kids were coming over) were going to be asking me about dinner in a matter of a few short hours.

I stopped matching socks.

As I glanced back at the TV one more time, I mused, "Thanks for the memories, Emeril. I can almost imagine what it would be like to have *someone else* preparing dinner for us tonight."

Now before you start thinking that I hate cooking, I don't. I love it, actually. What I truly don't like, however, is that feeling of dread that comes over me when I'm exhausted and it's 4 p.m. and I have no idea what's for dinner ... that's when I feel the stress level rise.

What you really want to cook up for breakfast is a huge serving of encouragement to get the day started off right. And if you serve that up with toast and jam, you're doing all right.

How often have you found yourself staring blankly into a cupboard or a freezer around dinner time, chastising yourself for forgetting to thaw the chicken? Nothing can send me over the edge like having to make dinner when I'm tired and uninspired. Can you relate?

Most of the time, the source of my frustration over meal time goes back to the core issue of time management. When I'm managing my time well, then I find I take advantage of the tools for time management in my kitchen as well as other areas of our home.

The kitchen is a gathering place. It should bring you joy, not angst! To be honest, when the kids were little, they preferred cereal for dinner. I think it's because it was the most consistent meal I served!

As our family has grown (both in number and age) I've learned a few things about managing our kitchen. Each year, I find I am enjoying cooking more and more. Don't get me wrong— I'm not going to pretend to be the Julia Childs of homeschooling—my goal is to encourage you to simplify mealtime so that your family enjoys both your company *and* the meal you prepare!

Up and At 'Em: Breakfast Shouldn't Be Burdensome

Have I mentioned that I am not a morning person? Well, I'm not. I spend the first few minutes of every day wondering what day it is and who all those children calling me "mom" are.

Now that you know this about me, you can see why making breakfast is not my strong suit. I have learned a few things though, that have really helped me get my breakfast groove on! First and foremost: we get up and eat together on purpose as often as we can. There are so many reasons to have breakfast together—morning is a great time to pray together, talk about the day's schedule, have devotions, and hang out before the busyness of the day sets in.

Breakfast Tip: Try making breakfast burritos ahead and freezing them. Voila! A healthy, easy morning meal!

If it's a school day, I'm less likely to get creative, because I prefer to put my energy into my favorite meal: dinner! I've found that on weekend mornings, when I don't feel the need to get school and laundry started simultaneously, I have more desire and energy to make a nice breakfast for the family. During the school week though, it's all about survival!

I'd like to tell you that I've got some sort of amazing breakfast routine down, but most weekday mornings, I end up setting out boxes of cereal and some yogurt to get us going. For some reason, I spent many years feeling guilty about this and then it occurred to me: the only one complaining about my lack of breakfast skills was... you guessed it ... me!

As it turns out, cereal and yogurt for breakfast do the trick just fine. Go easy on yourself, Mom! What you really want to cook up for breakfast is a huge serving of encouragement to get the day started off right. And if you serve that up with toast and jam, you're doing all right.

Tools of the Trade

Over the years I have come to rely on a few things in my kitchen that I can't imagine being without. Of course, I've also purchased many things that have ended up in a garage sale or in the garbage, too!

Let me start by listing a few must-haves. Every busy mom I know should have these things in her kitchen if at all possible:

Slow Cookers

When you think of slow cookers do you think of casseroles and church potlucks? If so, you're in for a treat, because slow cooker cooking has come a long way! In fact, I love my slow cooker! I use it for breakfast and dinner. Our slow cooker has been a friend to me over the years. I find that it is used more in the winter and the fall than summer months but it is the one item that I would choose over *any other appliance* in my kitchen for one reason: it makes me feel like a homemaking superstar!

Use Your Slow Cooker For Breakfast

Did you know you can cook breakfast in your slow cooker overnight and wake up to a wonderful warm meal? This is a busy homeschool mom's dream come true! I cook eggs, cobblers, oatmeal, and cereal recipes in my slow cooker overnight. It's amazing the breakfast ideas that are out there for slow cookers.

With some quick Internet searching over a weekend, you can create a menu for the week that will help you serve breakfast with a smile. We have made wonderful, hearty breakfast casseroles that are full of hash browns, breakfast meat, and more. Give it a try! You'll be glad you did.

The Busy Homeschool Mom Suggests

When purchasing a slow cooker, look for one with a removable dish. They are much easier to clean. I have also found that when I use a cooking bag to line the slow cooker, I have little to no cleanup. If you don't have a liner, you can spray the inside of the pot with cooking spray before you fill it to make cleanup easier.

Not sure where to start? Find a slow cooker cookbook or simply type in "slow cooker recipes" on the Internet and you will discover a plethora of frugal, time saving and absolutely delicious recipes.

Be on the lookout for what your family will

naturally gravitate towards. In our home, we love slow cooked beef, soups, and chicken. My favorite chicken recipe involves putting in frozen chicken around 10:00 a.m. and stirring every two hours or so. It's just what the doctor ordered!

You never know where you will find good recipes, either! The best recipe I ever found for roast beef was in a magazine that I was reading while sitting at my OB's office back in the late 90's. I still have that recipe. Who knew?

Pressure Cookers

Some moms I know still think of pressure cooking in terms of the old pressure cookers that they watched their grandmothers use. Most of the stories I heard about them came from my grandmother, too. She once had one blow up and break out a window!

Thank goodness that's not the case anymore. Today's pressure cookers are stylish and safe. I am a fan of electric pressure cookers. They look a lot like stylized slow cookers. I purchased one three years ago and I love it! Here's why:

It's fast

I can cook dried beans in about ¼ of the time.

This is especially wonderful for a busy mom like me, who tends to forget to soak beans overnight. Artichokes are done to perfection in just seven minutes!

From Frozen to Fabulous

A few years ago, I watched a chef as he put a frozen piece of chicken in the pressure cooker to make chicken parmesan in less than an hour. Being a mom who frequently forgot to thaw meat for dinner, I was instantly on board! This guy was so good that I decided to try his technique at home. I gave it a try and what do you know?! It worked! I simply layered frozen chicken breast in my pressure cooker with cheese and pasta, added spices and VOILA! From frozen to fabulous in less than an hour.

There is a learning curve to pressure cooking. It can take a little time to get used to using a pressure cooker, but once you do, I bet you'll be hooked. Flavorful meals, tender meats, delicate fish and chicken are done to perfection in minutes. Plus, pressure cooking makes it easy for even the busiest cooks to prepare meals from scratch, which saves money. Use your pressure cooker to make complete casserole style meals, or cook several foods at one time and have a home cooked meal on the table in minutes.

A word of caution: Not all pressure cookers are created equal. Do your homework. Read online reviews. Plan to buy one you'll love and use for years.

Now I realize that with my unsoaked beans and frozen chicken, it's starting to look like I forget to plan ahead sometimes. Okay. I do. But most of the time my family never knows it because I've learned to navigate my way around the kitchen in a hurry.

Time Saving Tip: Cook large batches of food and freeze what you don't use right away.

Freezer Meals (As in, I love to receive them)

I would love to tell you that I am adept at once-a-month cooking. But I'm not. I tried it for a few years and after that I wrestled with feeling guilty because I couldn't get the hang of it. It's funny how easily mommy-guilt can take hold, isn't it? For some reason, I thought that all good homeschool moms baked their own bread and made freezer meals!

Now, for those of you who love it, I applaud you

because YOU are my go-to girls for make ahead meals. I have been the grateful recipient of many freezer meals. This really is a great technique for many busy moms. There are wonderful freezer meal cookbooks available to purchase too—many are at your local library so you can take them for a test-drive before buying.

If you like the idea of freezer meals, you can try a simplified version of the idea. Whenever I'm making tacos or enchiladas, I like to make huge batches of seasoned chicken or ground beef and freeze the leftover meat. This has saved me hours and hours in the kitchen and it's great for taco night, or to add meat to simple pasta dishes, soups and stews. Keep it simple. Do what works for you!

Menu Planning

Menu planning is a wonderful tool. It doesn't have to be complicated, either. When I am really being diligent about planning my days, I try to include menu planning. If I spend just half an hour each week, I can plan meals for our family. It saves money and it brings so many benefits of health and peace into our home. The time I spend planning menus for our family is rewarded in so many ways.

If the idea of devising a menu plan for the week makes you roll your eyes because it sounds too exhausting, just think of the stress it will save you in the long run. I promise it's worth it! And you can deviate from it whenever you need to.

Often times, I make menus for just four nights out of seven because I know we'll either have breakfast for dinner, leftovers, or we'll be eating at a friend's house. Think of it like a schedule. Just having that menu there as a guide is a lifesaver.

Keep it simple, mom! You don't have to assign days to your meals.

One creative idea for menu planning is to create a very loose menu with three easy meals, two that are a bit more time consuming, an evening for leftovers or eating out, and one new recipe that you've been wanting to try. *Do your grocery shopping with these recipes in mind.* Menu planning does not mean that you have to assign days to your meals.

The beauty of planning for meals ahead of time is that if you have forgotten a dentist appointment late in the afternoon or you've had a busy week, everything you need for a quick meal is ready to go.

If the mealtime trifecta of time, energy and creativity hit

you at once, you can create one of the more time consuming dishes. *It's all about being flexible.*

Menu planning done right is a blessing—not a burden! My hunch is that if you sit down with a pencil and a paper, you will be able to knock out a simple menu plan and jot down a workable grocery list in 20 to 30 minutes. Give it a try by starting with a few things that you know your family enjoys. Before you know it, you'll have a menu!

Picky Eaters

I have a sign in my kitchen that says: "Menu Choices: Take It—Leave It". Our kids know that I am not a short-order cook. I cook for a large family and we all eat what is being served. Unless there is a food allergy involved, children are expected to eat what is served without complaining. This helps the children learn to at least try new things and it also keeps me from losing my mind trying to accommodate everyone's individual tastes.

Pizza night, of course, is still a huge hit with everyone, but our kids also enjoy many things that I never dreamed of eating as a child: steamed broccoli and curried chicken have become family favorites. Artichokes are served in season (thank you, pressure cooker) and the children have gradually become willing participants in *most* of my kitchen experiments. Gotta love them for that!

Also, remember to include the kids! Let them pick what they want for dinner on occasion. (It takes the guilt out of serving cereal when it's someone else's idea!) If you're worried they will choose meals that aren't as nutritious as you prefer, let them choose one dish, then add the veggies needed to round out the meal.

Teach Your Children how to Cook

As a teenager, I learned how to cook for my family of nine. My mom was working and I was the oldest daughter. For the most part I enjoyed cooking when I was given the opportunity. The only downside was that I grew up cooking in massive amounts! When Jay and I were married, I seriously did not know how to cook for just two people. When I made chili, it was "vat" sized. Mashed potato portions were usually big enough to serve at Thanksgiving Dinner. It was hilarious and handicapping at the same time.

Seeing my "supersized" cooking, my mother-in-law bought me my first cookbook about eight months after Jay and I were married. It was called "Cooking for Two." I still have it, because it makes me smile. And at some point, I am told, I will likely be cooking for two again. I am glad that my mom and my mother-in-law saw value in teaching me how to make meals for a family.

We have been part of a homeschool co-op for nearly thirteen years. In that time, I have seen dozens of cooking classes taught. Year after year, these classes fill up with students (boys and girls) who are eager to learn how to cook and bake. Many of these kids do not know basic kitchen techniques and cannot follow simple recipes. This shouldn't be the case.

Mom, take advantage of these eager learners. Most children love to help in the kitchen. By the time your children are in their teens, they should be able to cook complete meals on their own if necessary. In our home, there are a few easy dinners that the younger kids (ages 8-11) know how to make. Our older kids can make almost anything with a little supervision to "finesse" a recipe along.

Enlisting young kids to help with cooking also makes children very aware of what goes into dinner preparation. I have a dinner helper or two each night. One child is assigned to help me prepare the meal while another one sets the table and prepares the dining room. We interact together while I cook and teach.

Not only is it a worthwhile investment in your children, but if you have high schoolers, you can use the credit for school. Remember Home Ec? Cooking with your kids is a great opportunity for you to build a deeper relationship around a simmering pot of stew or a ball of dough. Eventually, you will work yourself out of a job in the kitchen! I know that I am blessed beyond measure when my older children take it upon themselves to cook and clean in the kitchen.

Lazy Lunches and Leftovers

I don't know about you, but lunch is my *least* favorite meal to prepare. The old PB&J gets very boring and I like to spend my energy on dinner plans. However! Don't forget about leftovers! Using leftovers during lunch can save you time and energy, and kids love them.

When you're deciding what to cook for dinner, think about how you might incorporate leftovers into a lunch for the following day. Make a few extra servings for dinner and set them aside for the next day's lunch.

Here are a few ideas for making it work:

- ❖ If you had tacos for dinner, set aside some of the cooked meat. Use it the next day in quesadillas. I have gotten very creative with these and the kids love them with refried beans, shredded chicken and cheese. Ten minutes and you're done!

- ❖ If you make chicken breasts, prepare an extra serving and slice it for sandwiches the next day instead of purchasing deli lunch meat.

- ❖ If you're making a salad for dinner, slice some extra vegetables, such as cucumbers, carrots, bell peppers, and celery, or make an extra undressed salad for yourself after dinner for the next day.

- ❖ While you're making dinner, boil a few eggs. These are full of protein and can be served alone or in salads and sandwiches.

- ❖ Make extra pasta, couscous, or rice and make side salads for lunch by cutting up vegetables and adding salad dressing.

- ❖ Cold pasta salad is easy to make with leftover pasta—add olives, veggies and salad dressing and you're done!

- ❖ Grill extra vegetables and use them in sandwiches.
- ❖ Make an extra baked potato and pack it with nutritious toppings.

If you're worried that dinner might seem less appealing the following day, consider serving it for lunch two days later, provided the food will remain fresh for an extra day. Most of the time, it will keep just fine.

What are some things that you know your whole family loves that are also easy? Here are a few of our family favorites. I make at least one of these options once a week—great for nights when we have to be somewhere or we're just tired and I don't want to think about cooking.

- ❖ Quesadillas
- ❖ Grilled cheese sandwiches
- ❖ Taco bar
- ❖ Spaghetti
- ❖ Taco soup (I make this in huge batches. It freezes well and is even better for lunch the next day!)
- ❖ Hamburgers
- ❖ Potato soup

Honey, Can We Go Out For Dinner?

Several years ago, my husband bought me a cute magnet from a gift store in Cannon Beach, Oregon. I still love it. Here's what it says:

"THE WAY TO A WOMAN'S HEART IS THROUGH THE DOOR OF A RESTAURANT."

Now I know it's tongue-in-cheek but it sure makes me smile, because *nothing* says "I love you" like my husband offering to bring home a pizza on his way home from the office, especially after I've had a hard day at home.

Take-out means I don't have many dishes to do and I don't have to plan a thing.

Busy homeschool mom, it's okay to give yourself a break every now and then. In fact, I think it's something you should do regularly if you can. You don't need to feel guilty about opting for a take-out meal that everyone will like.

Look at it this way: if the occasional Chinese food take-out saves your sanity, it will be worth far more than the cost of the meal!

Make It the Best Time of the Day

No matter how your meal comes to the table, I encourage you to really endeavor to make mealtimes special. Light candles. Put a vase of flowers on the table. Teach your children to set the table properly.

Make this time at the end of your day a time to talk and catch up with each other no matter how old or young your children are. Some of the best conversations we have as a family are around the dinner table. For that reason alone, putting time and energy into mealtime is a worthy undertaking.

As your children grow, mealtimes will become part of the tapestry of special memories they will have from their growing up years.

CHAPTER 5

Discouraged Daylight

IF AT FIRST YOU DON'T SUCCEED . . .
TRY, TRY AGAIN

The Lord will guide you continually,
and satisfy your needs in parched places...
~ Isaiah 58:11

Homeschool moment of the week: Our eight-year old finished her math test the other day and surprised me by scoring much higher than I expected. I was feeling very good about my stellar math teaching skills when she announced, "Wow! Guessing really DOES work!"

Ah, homeschooling. If it doesn't bring you to your knees, nothing will!

I love to speak to homeschool moms. There is something about being able to bring encouragement to another mom that sets my spirit soaring. I think it's because I understand feeling overwhelmed and discouraged. I have also experienced the grace and mercy of God in my life. I am a witness to the fact that His strength is made perfect in weakness.

Homeschooling has exposed so many more weaknesses than I ever knew I had! If I even thought for a moment I was a patient person, I have learned otherwise. I have bad days, days that I stay in my pajamas, days that make me question why I'm homeschooling and days that I question my sanity for that matter! Ask any of my girlfriends or even my kids. They'll back me up on this one!

I'm so glad I know the Lord. His strength really is made perfect in weakness. It's true! Check out what Paul says in 2 Corinthians:

> "BUT HE SAID TO ME, 'MY GRACE IS SUFFICIENT FOR YOU, FOR MY POWER IS MADE PERFECT IN WEAKNESS.' THEREFORE I WILL BOAST ALL THE MORE GLADLY ABOUT MY WEAKNESSES, SO THAT CHRIST'S POWER MAY REST ON ME."
> 2 CORINTHIANS 12:9

Don't you love that? God wants to receive glory from our weakness, because when we boast in our weakness, His power *actually rests* on us. Who wouldn't want that?

You've got real, God-given bragging rights here, mom! You get to boast about your weaknesses, and then watch as His strength is made perfect through them. We serve an amazing God.

He cares about even the smallest detail of my day! I'm learning that as I purpose to accomplish what God has put before me in a way that honors Him, He comes through. I'm learning to rely on our amazing God more and more.

If God has put homeschooling before you, trust Him! He has already equipped you for the job!

You can tap into God's power too, busy homeschool mom! In the book of Matthew we see a call to persistent prayer:

> **"ASK AND IT WILL BE GIVEN TO YOU;**
> **SEEK AND YOU WILL FIND; KNOCK AND**
> **THE DOOR WILL BE OPENED TO YOU."**
> **MATTHEW 7:7**

Do you feel overwhelmed by the task of homeschooling? His strength is made perfect in weakness.

Are you asking? Are you seeking?

Jesus tells us that true wisdom, discernment, and strength only come from God—and only God can give the understanding that will enable us to do what He puts before us. If He has put homeschooling before you, trust Him! He has already equipped you for the job!

I love being a child of the King. I love the way He loves me. He is patient. He is a God of mercies which are *new every day*. Your day matters to God. He cares about the details of your day—after all, He created you! So if you're not doing so already, I want to encourage you to bring your challenges and concerns before the Lord and wait expectantly on Him.

He will help you. Consider what David says in Psalm 18:1:

> ## "IN MY DISTRESS I CALLED TO THE LORD; I CRIED TO MY GOD FOR HELP. FROM HIS TEMPLE HE HEARD MY VOICE; MY CRY CAME BEFORE HIM, INTO HIS EARS."

Verses like this give me strength because they remind me that God hears my cries for help—and He's clearly used to hearing cries like mine! So right down to the curriculum you choose, cry out to God for help. He is still with us today. He is our true source of power and strength.

By now I hope you have banished any thought of trying to be a "supermom" and replaced thoughts of doubt with a picture of a woman who is constantly aware of her dependence on the Lord.

Don't give up. Give in to Him.

Just Say It

Not too long ago, I logged on to Facebook and saw the status update of a friend who had eight children and who had been homeschooling for over ten years. "I quit," it read. "All of our children are being sent to public school starting on Monday." That's all it said, but it sent shockwaves through our homeschool community.

We need to say it when we're struggling—and we need to be grace-filled listeners!

Some homeschool moms who read the status and were just hanging on by a thread themselves felt discouraged by the post, even jealous. But there was nothing to be jealous of. No amount of free time was worth what my precious friend was going through in private.

Every day after that for about a week, she gave little

glimpses into what had ultimately convinced her and her husband to put all their kids into public school. The main reason was that she felt her relationships with her children were suffering because of homeschooling. Homeschooling had taken over her life, leaving her bitter and frustrated, tired and angry.

But you'd never know it. They sure looked good on the outside; kids were well dressed and polite at the co-op. Mom was always sharing recipe ideas and letting us in on her homemaking secrets. She seemed so happy. In fact, it was very intimidating to be around her!

Her "perfect" homeschool life, as it turned out, wasn't perfect at all. In fact, she was working so hard to keep up the facade that she nearly lost her marriage. She was stressed out and discouraged. In private, her children were rebellious and disrespectful.

Here's the part that makes this cautionary tale so, well—cautionary: She never said a thing to anyone about it. Her struggle was in private and so was her pain. She was isolated to the point of being an emotional sitting duck. Satan loves it when we are isolated, because isolation is a killer. My friend needed real, honest encouragement from other moms who would have prayed for her and identified with her.

Unfortunately, because she was so afraid of what others would say if they *really* knew her, she was unable to glean wisdom and perspective from other moms who could identify with her and pray for her.

In the end, it might not have made a difference, but my guess is that it probably would have. Most of the time, this kind of painful burnout can be avoided if we just say it when we're struggling rather than avoiding the people who are most likely to understand what we're going through.

> Most of the time, moms who are on the verge of burnout are afraid to say so because they live in abject fear of being judged by others.
>
> Oh that we would be known for our grace toward one another!

We need to say it when we're struggling—and we need to be grace-filled listeners! Most of the time, moms who are on the verge of burnout don't say so because they live in abject fear of what others will say to them or even worse–about them—if they show any weakness or doubt in their lives. Oh that we would be known for our grace toward one another!

So how are *you* doing, mom?

Do you lack self-control? Say it.

Do you need help with homeschooling? Say it.

Are you discouraged? Say it.

Is your marriage suffering? Say it.

Do you have a difficult child? Say it?

Is your family struggling to stay afloat? Say it!

Could you be more grace-filled as a friend? Say it!

Turns out that we are much more of an encouragement to others when we are honest about the way life really is. That means we share our struggles, not just our successes.

We need to bear one another's burdens.

BEAR ONE ANOTHER'S BURDENS, AND SO FULFILL THE LAW OF CHRIST.
GALATIANS 6:2

This is why relationships with other homeschool moms are so important. It is our duty as believers to help bear one another's burdens. When we see a friend stagger, we help steady the load. If she is struggling, we help bear the burden. And if she stumbles, we lift her up. Helping others is one of the defining marks of mature Christian character.

Blessed are the Flexible ... for they shall not break

Do you remember gym class when you were ten years old? I do. I could do the "splits" in 5th grade. In fact, I could do them all the way through high school, because I challenged myself to stay flexible. It was a requirement for the sport I had chosen. Every day, I stretched my muscles, pushing myself to do better in order to stay at the top of my game and be an asset my teammates.

> **flex·i·ble**
> adj [flek-suh-buhl]
> 1: capable of being flexed : pliant
> 2: yielding to influence
> 3: characterized by a ready capability to adapt to new, different, or changing requirements ie: <a flexible schedule>
> adaptable, adjustable, alterable, changeable, elastic, fluid, malleable, modifiable, pliable, variable, adaptable, adjustable, alterable, changeable, elastic, fluid, malleable, modifiable, pliable, variable

Stretching did not seem important to me when I first started. Like many of my teammates, I cut corners and arrived late to practice a few times. But eventually it caught up with me. I learned the hard way that when I did not stretch before a game or a competition, I was likely to pay dearly for it. Torn muscles, aches, poor performance and even injury were the end result of a lack of flexibility. Staying flexible was not only an exercise in self-discipline, it was essential to the success of our team.

The ability to flex with life is what most successful homeschool moms have in common.

"Use it or lose it!" Those were the words I heard most often from my coach. I bet if she had known I was going to grow up to be a homeschool mom, she would have trained me harder. I sure use those same principles now in many areas of life.

The "use it or lose it" approach still works for me now as a busy homeschool mom. If I stop being flexible and become rigid or unyielding to the seasons and changing circumstances in our family, I lose my ability to be flexible. Just like my team from high school suffered when I did not commit to a mindset of being prepared and flexible, our entire family suffers when I neglect this important principle of daily life.

Yes, homeschooling requires flexibility. For that matter, parenting requires flexibility. When we are both primary educator for our children and parent, we need to be ready to meet the challenges that will inevitably come our way from day to day.

The *ability to flex with life* is what most successful homeschool moms have in common.

I love Webster's® definition of flexible: "characterized by a ready capability to adapt to new, different or changing requirements."

In fact, every day, I find I am learning something new about what works and what doesn't. If each day is different, then I should not be surprised that each year will be different, too!

For example, two years ago, I had a high school senior, a preschooler, a new driver, and a new jr. higher. This year, I have a college student, a high school senior (round two), a freshman and an infant! What worked for me two years ago will definitely not work right now.

I can feel myself streeeeettchinnngggg as I write this, because it's taken me almost a year to complete a manuscript that I desperately wanted to have done months ago! The reality of my life right now is that I simply don't have eight hours a day to devote to writing. My season of life requires that I write when I can, not when I want to.

Are you flexible? Would your children characterize you as able to "flow with it" when it comes to changing circumstances and new challenges?

If not, give it a try. Add "adaptable, adjustable, changeable, malleable, modifiable and elastic" to the list of words that could describe you. Heck. You can even try adding "rubbery" and "stretchy" to your list of desired character qualities if it will help put a smile on your face and flexibility on your radar. Give it a try.

Do-over, Please!

The other day, a few of our older children were laughing hysterically about something as they sat around the living room. As I leaned in to listen, I realized that they were laughing at me! Turns out some of my "near misses" as a mother are great fodder for jokes later in life. Yes, it's true. Our kids have been gracious guinea pigs in my homeschool and parenting laboratory on more than one occasion. We laugh now, but it wasn't always funny!

In fact, I have tried what feels like a gazillion things that didn't work. For example, there was the year I tried to double up on morning chores in an effort to have more free time in the afternoon. FAIL. I'm surprised that my two older girls (both of whom now appear to be at least mostly recovered) are still speaking to me given the fact that I persisted in this pattern for several months and only stopped because more than three children were crying at one time. I needed a do-over.

Do-overs are wonderful. They are especially good if you give yourself permission to stop what you're doing and actually start over instead of persisting in a pattern that's not working for you.

Then there was the MASTER schedule. I call it the "master" because it *was* the master; we were nothing but slaves to it! In the spring of 2003, I attempted this VERY complicated "master" schedule and it just about killed my husband.

It was an innocent experiment, really. I had read a wonderful book on scheduling and I was honestly trying to make things easier! Instead, I drove everyone up a tree. I was scheduling our family from 6:00 a.m. to 10:00 p.m.—even scheduling in "alone" time with Jay! Can you imagine? (Well, it seemed like a good idea at the time.)

Anyway!

As you can imagine this left us very little time for spontaneous interaction (see my first book, *The Busy Homeschool Mom's Guide to Romance* on White Space) and it really put a damper on our love life (to say the least).

However! That color-coded schedule *did look amazing* hanging on the wall. It even impressed the ever-present homeschool nay-sayers that came over for the occasional holiday dinner or birthday party. I will confess, I liked that part.

The bad part was that I was practically married to that schedule. (See, "MASTER.") It made me feel guilty every time I looked at it and it didn't match up with the clock. The "formula" seemed so great at the time—but as the needs of our family changed, the schedule didn't. I had invested so much time and energy into the schedule that the idea of scrapping it made me feel like a failure. So I just kept right on making the best of it.

Slowly, I began to realize I wasn't asking the right questions.

The right question was, "Lord, what do YOU have for me?" but I was so busy trying to implement my schedule, I forgot to pencil God in!

No wonder I was on the verge of burning out! I had set a pace for myself that was virtually impossible to maintain. I was not allowing God to be in control of my days. I was trying to do it myself.

I needed someone to give me permission to wipe the slate clean and start again. I needed a do-over.

I praise the Lord for the loving interactions that I am blessed to share with my husband, particularly when I need fresh perspective. As I became more and more discouraged, he was watching. One night after dinner, I finally admitted to Jay that things were not going nearly as smoothly as our beautifully laid out schedule made it appear.

While he appeared shocked (He's so good to me...), I soon discovered that he wasn't.

"Look at it, Jay!" I said as I pointed to the schedule. "I mean, really! It's mocking me from the front of the refrigerator! The MASTER has me beat... and it *knows* it does!" Jay tried not to let his half-smile show. (Clearly, I was losing my mind.) The children began to clean off the table more quickly. I'm sure they thought I was going to blow like the volcano we were studying in science every Tuesday and Thursday at 1:00 p.m. Sharp.

Patient, sweet man that I married, his soft heart and knowing smile softened my defensive posture. He knew how much I wanted that schedule to work. I began to load the dishwasher while the kids got ready for bed. As I worked, Jay began asking me questions about our routine. After a while, he took the schedule off the refrigerator and we looked at it together.

By the way, dads:

Your wife does not need you to fix everything that she talks to you about. Most of the time, she just needs to know that her struggles matter to you. She needs to know that you're interested. And she needs the occasional "get out of the house free" card in the form of a drive through Starbucks or a solo trip to the grocery store. Don't make it as complicated as she does.

We depend on you to simplify things. Really.

Jay listened to me for at least two hours that night. I was so glad to have someone to talk to about my frustration in this area! Just knowing that he was interested seemed to lift part of the burden. Once we looked it over, it became clear that a large part my problem was unrealistic expectations, both for myself and for the children.

Jay encouraged me to release my death grip from the MASTER, and try to become more flexible as a wife and mother. His simple encouragement set me free from my self-imposed sentence of discouragement and defeat over my own unmet expectations.

"Hey, babe," my husband suggested, "What if you just did the basics until you settle into a better routine with the baby? What if you got out of the house a couple mornings a week for a change of scenery? I say you do *more* things that you'll all enjoy... but don't schedule it. Just go with the flow. If it works to take a walk, take one."

"What?! But our routine will fall apart," I wailed.

"Yeah," he said. "And it's about time. Because when you're not in a good place, no one else in our home is, either."

Ouch. I mean, really! Ouch! But I knew he was right. Busy Homeschool Mom, you are the temperature taker for your home. Have you ever heard that old saying, "If mama ain't happy, ain't nobody happy"? Boy, isn't that the truth. The tone in our home was grumpy and tense. And everyone knew it, but I was really the only one who could do anything to change it. The ball was in my court.

I had fallen into the homeschool vortex and I was seriously stuck in there. I couldn't see the schooling that was happening in every day life because I was so worried about getting everything done just right and according to schedule. Come to think of it, I still struggle with this area of my life! I am constantly having to give my plans to the Lord and ask for His guidance and forgiveness. It's part of walking with Him.

Thank God that He allows do-overs. We need them.

Failure, You Are a Friend of Mine

If you have tried a bazillion different things in your homeschool, you're not alone. In fact, you're in very good company. One of the best things that ever happened to our homeschool, in fact, was hearing from other moms who had been on the journey longer than me and who had experienced a certain level of, well, failure.

Turns out, failure is an essential part of success. This is true in every area of life but it's particularly important in the area of homeschooling. Failure sends us back to the drawing board.

> You need to be okay with failure. Let it teach you instead of allowing it to taunt you. Really, that's the accuser of your soul at the end of the day.
>
> His is the voice that would have you give up, but God says, "You can do all things through Christ!"
>
> Philippians 4:13

I have heard it argued that admitting to our weakness only encourages complacency, but I disagree. Knowing that other moms struggle does not encourage me. However! Hearing other moms talk about the failures they have experienced in the light of the success they finally found does.

Successful homeschool moms do experience failure! But

they do not let failure defeat them *or* define them.

A friend of mine recently sent me this photo in an email:

S u c c e s s

What people think it looks like.

What it really looks like.

Isn't this GREAT? It's so freeing to know that success takes time. The road to success is quite often a bumpy one! It means trying new things, letting go of things that do not work and always looking for ways to improve things.

So if you are trying a routine that's not working for you, feel free to throw it out! Start over. And next year, you may decide to try a new method. You need to be okay with failure. Let it teach you instead of allowing it to taunt you. Really, that's the accuser of your soul at the end of the day. His is the voice that would have you give up.

God says you can do ALL THINGS.

Feeling stiff and unbending? Exercise your ability to flex with changing circumstances. Be purposeful about it.

Dinner menu killing you? Simplify it! You don't need to be Rachel Ray right now. Your kids are happy with Carol Brady and Mac-n-Cheese nights. Besides, as a good friend just pointed out to me, Carol Brady had Alice! Sometimes I want an "Alice", too!

Outside activities making you cringe? Pare them down.

Curriculum burdensome? Stop using it. Ask God for His heart in helping you find a curriculum that works for your family. Remember, it should help you, not cripple and overwhelm you.

Feeling defeated? Ask the Lord to help you see yourself through the lens of His precious Son! You CAN do all things through Christ!

> ## "I CAN DO ALL THINGS THROUGH CHRIST WHO STRENGTHENS ME."
> ### PHILIPPIANS 4:13

Are you at the end of your rope? Tie a knot and hang on! Nothing worth doing in this life is ever easy. Homeschooling is worth the sacrifice when we yield our will to His. We know that we will reap good fruit if we wait on the Lord and trust His promises. That's right! Good things are coming!

I'll leave you with the words Paul spoke to the people of Galatia in Galatians 6:9. This verse has been taped to just about every surface in my house over the years because it reminds me to stay the course:

> "AND LET US NOT GROW WEARY WHILE DOING GOOD, FOR IN DUE SEASON WE SHALL REAP IF WE DO NOT LOSE HEART."
> GALATIANS 6:8-10

The harvest is coming, Mom! Don't lose heart.

CHAPTER 6

Consolidated Daylight

MULTI-LEVEL TEACHING

Education is not the filling of a pail but the lighting of a fire.
~ William Butler Yeats

Have you ever had a moment like this?

Picture a mom in her bedroom—on her knees amidst laundry and paperwork, crying out to the Lord, "Help! I'm overwhelmed! I want to quit! Surely this was not what You had in mind when you asked me to homeschool. Please tell me it wasn't."

This was me, five years into homeschooling. With a jr. higher, a middle schooler, a 4th grader, 2nd grader, and a Kinder, I was in over my head. Or at least it felt like that. My life was consumed by homeschooling. "No wonder people think we're crazy!" I thought. "Because this is a little on the 'crazy' side of things!"

Homeschooling *one* child can make a homeschool mom feel a little nutty ... and without a plan for success, homeschooling several grade levels can open the door wide to a place I call the "Homeschool Vortex." Believe me, it's not a place I like to hang out for very long. I knew I needed to simplify if we were going to be successful at homeschooling long term.

For our family, simplifying meant learning how to teach multiple levels at once. Since I had to start somewhere, I began to look at what was already within my reach. I was fairly organized. (check!) I had compelling reasons to improve (check!) and I wasn't afraid to learn something new—to think outside of my workbooks and checklists. (*ahem* ... check!)

After weeks of researching various homeschooling styles, I decided upon one that really seemed to fit our multi-level homeschool. I was very intrigued by unit studies in combination with notebooking. Here is why this approach interested me:

Many years ago, I discovered something that most

seasoned homeschool moms I knew had already figured out: the more children we had, the less of me there was to go around. Often, I was homeschooling from morning until just before dinner—and sometimes long after dinner was over. I was frustrated. To make matters worse, since the kids were all in different grades, they were all studying different areas of history and science. Talk about complicated! Even our timeline was confusing, with one student studying the Civil War and another ancient Mayan culture.

Since the kids were all in different grades, they were all studying different areas of history and science.

Something had to give. Since we had committed to homeschooling indefinitely, I knew I had to figure out a way to go the distance. At the rate we were traveling down the homeschool highway, we were headed for burnout. I could feel it.

We also dreamed of something *more* from our homeschool experience. In all honesty, we were tired. The children felt the stress too. I yearned for more *life* in our homeschooling. I just wasn't sure how to find it. I'd heard of unit studies, and frankly, the idea intimidated me. But, with a little encouragement from my husband, other moms and the internet, I began to shift my thinking from tutoring each child individually to a more family centered learning mentality.

Since we were mid-way through the year, it was a good time to take a break. I took the kids to the library, and we came home with our usual "wagonload" of books. I figured this would keep the kids busy while I sought the Lord as to how we were going to find a new way to homeschool. As always, my time with the Lord revealed areas where I could definitely improve.

Method vs. Manner

The first thing the Lord impressed on my heart during this time was that I needed to take a good hard look at the *manner* in which I was teaching the kids, so I did the only reasonable thing to do: I asked my older kids what they thought of our homeschooling. Specifically, I wanted to know their honest opinion of the job I was doing as their teacher.

From their candid answers, I learned two things:

- ❖ My manner of teaching was frustrating our kids.
- ❖ The methods I was using weren't working in the way I wanted them to.

"Apparently," our kids saw me as this ultra-stressed out homeschool mom. Who knew? It turns out that the stress I was feeling was affecting every area of our lives at home. We had gone from being excited about homeschooling to dreading it. I was on overload and I was passing that sense of feeling overwhelmed on to the kids.

We needed more LIFE in our homeschool. Less fragmented learning. More time together. Less individual study. More purpose-driven lessons, less "busy work". I began to seek the Lord for ways to bring this kind of life into our homeschooling. As I spent time in prayer and with our kids, I began to discover a whole new way of looking at our homeschool.

We needed more LIFE in our homeschool.

Turns out that the "life" we were needing was right in front of us. Since one of our goals in homeschooling was to instill in our children a real love of learning, I began to look into options that took me outside of my "comfort zone." I started checking into literature-based curricula, and loved what I found. It turned out that history and science could easily be taught using a "one room schoolroom" approach.

I was encouraged. And then, it came to me. Jay and I wanted to:

❖ Learn together
❖ Incorporate individual studies into our daily routine
❖ Focus on relationships
❖ Engage our children each day far beyond academic pursuits

LIFE. The simple spelling of this word gave me four key elements to teaching a houseful successfully. I started by ditching the four different history books and four different science workbooks in favor of one living history book, Bible reading, a missionary story, and one excellent science book. When I found the books I was looking for, we began to study together in the mornings.

I was amazed at how much more time this approach allowed us! Even though we were studying the same things, the children were given age-appropriate assignments, which opened up many more discussions about school during the day. The older kids were engaging the younger ones, too! It was what we were praying for. Not without its struggles but far better than what we had been doing.

We also began notebooking. Notebooking allowed the children to express their creative side and to demonstrate their understanding of what we were studying. It was exciting to see our 9th grader and our 3rd grader studying the same subject. It added to the experience of learning more than I ever dreamed it would.

L—Learning Together

Notebooking allowed me to further consolidate our learning experience. Here is how it worked for us: As soon as we switched from individual subject, workbook-based learning to a more family-integrated approach, I noticed a difference in the way the children approached school. We were learning together.

I soon realized that I could take the day's history lesson and give the older kids a writing assignment that was based on it while the younger ones colored a picture or did a craft related to the same subject. Voila! Two birds with one stone.

After a while, we began illustrating what we were learning. Our oldest children loved the creativity and I loved watching them come up with ways to write and illustrate a science lesson or a highlight from a missionary biography or history lesson we were reading.

I- Individual Subjects: Just Three

Of course, we can't study all the core subjects together. But essentially, there are really only three that cannot be studied as a group:

- ❖ Math
- ❖ Reading
- ❖ Handwriting

These are the subjects that I spend individual time with each child studying. Often times I will make a handwriting assignment part of a history lesson or a science concept using copy work. But in these three areas, each child is at a different level.

Because we were studying so many things together each morning, I found that I had enough time to spend with individual children and finish up before 2:00. Multi-level teaching also gave me time to focus on what I have come to believe is the most important part of homeschooling: personal relationships.

F- Focus on Relationships

We live in a culture that has largely forgotten the importance of nurturing relationships within the family. Our culture embraces a Greek model of education—but I have become a big believer in taking some *elements* of a Greek model and incorporating them into a Jewish approach to education. The Jewish culture was known for its emphasis on mentoring and discipleship.

As we became more entwined as a family, I found we had more time to mentor and disciple our children. This is the true benefit and opportunity of homeschooling. And multi-level teaching provides a wonderful backdrop for it.

E—Engage Your Children

I was watching Letterman a few years ago and there was a guest on the show who was talking about the decline of amazement in our culture. "Everything's amazing and nobody's happy," he said.

These words are so true! We live in a time of incredible technological advancement and yet, nobody's happy with it—the internet signal is "too slow" and the cell phone signal is too weak. We can fly from Oregon to New York in a day but instead of being amazed at the ability to fly at 35,000 feet all the way to NY, we complain about the leg room. I often tell our kids—next time you fly, look out the window and yell, "LOOK! We're FLYING!!!" and see what happens. Not really—but you get what I mean.

We are used to beautiful sunsets with dazzling colors. Animals of every conceivable kind roam the earth. Amazing signs of God's creativity are on display everywhere we look. Yet for all the wonder that surrounds us, we often fail to stop and simply marvel at it all.

Do you want to get your child excited about learning? Then teach him to be *amazed*. Engage your children by making a point to just talk about the wonderful things around you that God has made. Engage them in conversation. Ask them what they think God might have been thinking when He designed an elephant or an African grey parrot. (Now there's an amazing creature!)

Stop and study the parts of a flower that you find in the park. Talk about the sounds that birds make. Engage your children and teach them to be amazed. Write about what you see—draw pictures of flowers and birds and even slugs! They're amazing, too!

The Gift that Keeps on Giving

One of the many benefits of homeschooling is the time that it gives families to experience LIFE together. Don't take it for granted. You are training children of the King! There is no greater privilege.

Enjoy it. Soak it up. Squeeze as much amazement as you can out of the homeschool years. Ask the Lord to show you what LIFE for *your family* looks like and then trust Him. The journey you're on is a journey worth enjoying together.

CHAPTER 7

Wasted Daylight

VIRTUAL REALITY

Even if you are on the right track,
you'll get run over if you just sit there.
~ Will Rogers

Do you remember the first email you ever received? I sure do! I was a young mother at the time and my best friend from college called me to announce she was trying something new called "Juno."

It all sounded ridiculous but Margaret said that if I downloaded the software, she could communicate with me almost instantaneously via the computer. Well, why not? After a few hours of trying to figure it out, I called my husband in (the first of what has undoubtedly become thousands of 'please fix the computer' calls), and shortly thereafter *kapow!* my first email arrived.

I believe it said something like this: "Hi Heidi! Are you there? It's me, Margaret!" I was amazed. And I was hooked.

We've come a long way since then, haven't we? The convenience of the internet has come with benefits—and disadvantages. Now, I average about two-hundred emails a day.

Nearly everything that's for sale can be found online; from curriculum to slow cooker recipes, the internet has put the world at our fingertips. I can manage my banking with the touch of a button or download a book to my iPad. I can even watch how-to videos on everything from cooking to calligraphy via YouTube! From lapbooking to math problems, if I need an answer, I can find it online.

Gotta love that. And I do love it! Like most busy homeschool moms, I've got several favorite educational sites that I visit. I keep a blog. And I love my Facebook. Yes sir, I love me some Facebook.

I wish I didn't sometimes.

As you have probably figured out by now, there's a dark side to the internet. The more obvious dangers include internet pornography and the increasingly common problem of identity theft. Our kids are at greater risk for being exposed to things we could not have imagined before the dawn of the internet age. Predators target young children through search engines and social media.

Social networking sites abound. Opportunities to reconnect with old friends and make new ones entice even busy homeschool moms online every day. See if you can relate to this scenario:

7:00 a.m. I'm up a little ahead of my kids.

7:05 a.m. I decide to check my email.

7:25 After answering a plethora of morning emails, I wake the children. I greet them and while I throw my laundry into the washer, announce that we have a lot to get done, so they better hurry and get dressed.

TICK TOCK.

7:30 Kids are waking up, so I grab my laptop while I make breakfast and I get on Facebook to see what's going on with 1700 of my closest friends and relatives.

8:00 a.m. I follow a link to a recipe my friend has posted that looks like it might be a great option for Thanksgiving dinner in a few months. Then I go back to Facebook to comment to my friend about her great link. Turns out she is online, too. A chat window pops up on my screen. I can't say "no" to a great chance to catch up.

TICK TOCK.

We talk about old times. I upload pictures of my kids and send them to her. She sends me pictures of her new house ... and on it goes.

TICK TOCK.

10:30 a.m. finds me irritated as it takes me *completely* by surprise.

I respond by yelling at the kids.

"Why isn't anyone doing their schoolwork? Whose day is it to unload the dishwasher? Why aren't the beds made?" I yell. "Why can't you kids ever just get going on your own? Why do I always have to tell you what to do when you all know what you're supposed to be doing? The schedule is right on the kitchen wall for everyone to see!"

I sigh. Loudly. The kids sheepishly begin their morning chores while I mutter about how irresponsible everyone is. As I am getting school work organized, my cell phone texts me a calendar reminder. I pick up the phone and visualize all the plans I had made for the day evaporate as I am reminded about the dentist appointment that we have to be at in less than an hour.

And to top it all off, I know in my heart that *I'm the one to blame.*

Can I get a witness?

It's wasted daylight. And in reality, it's not my day to waste. It's the Lord's.

I don't start out each day wanting to waste my time. In fact, the opposite is true. But I've come to believe that when I consistently get caught up in things like Facebook (or whatever the distraction may be), there are two issues in play: self control and stewardship.

Self Control: Choosing to be Filled with the Spirit

> BUT THE FRUIT OF THE SPIRIT IS LOVE,
> JOY, PEACE, PATIENCE, KINDNESS,
> GOODNESS, FAITHFULNESS, GENTLENESS,
> SELF-CONTROL; AGAINST SUCH THINGS
> THERE IS NO LAW.
> GALATIANS 5:22-23

Do you remember a series of records that were released for kids in the 1980's called "The Music Machine?" In one of their albums, there was a song about self-control. As a child,

I listened to these over and over and I still remember most of the songs about the fruit of the spirit.

In one song, the children sang:

Self-control, is just controlling yourself. It's listening to your heart—and doing what is smart.

Don't you love that? It's simple, because it was written for children but it is so true!

We live in a society that is plagued by a lack of self-control. One only has to tune into the local news to hear about the latest pastor or politician whose career has been decimated and lost due to a lack of self-control.

Self-control, is just controlling yourself ...

It's easy to see the destructive consequences of public loss of self-control. However, consistent lack of self-control is not benign. Lack of self-control is as old as sin itself. It was even the root cause of Solomon's undoing as a godly king. When we don't have self-control in our marriages, they suffer. When we lack personal self-control in our homeschool, our children suffer and we become an easy target for the enemy to come in and whisper, "You can't do this. Look how many things you've started and never finished."

It's listening to your heart, and doing what is smart ...

At the end of the day, without self-control, we open ourselves up to the bitter taste of regret and wasted opportunities.

There's a particular reason that self-control is the last fruit of the Spirit listed by Paul in Galatians 5. Without self-control, the other fruits are hindered, especially if we allow our own desires to usurp the direction of the Spirit.

For me, the internet has been both friend and foe. I use it for research, for communication and for homeschooling, just to name a few things. It also provides me with a constant test of my personal self-control. In fact, as I am writing this book, the constant "ding" of an incoming email is a huge distraction. I have to ask the Lord specifically to help me stay at the task He has called me to. I must keep right on writing, choosing to ignore the email until the time is right to read it. I have a choice to make. I can either waste my precious free time in the evening on Facebook or watching television, or I can redeem the time.

When the temptation is too much, I may need to disconnect the wireless for a while so I'm not distracted. Or, I may need to go somewhere quiet where there is no internet access. Choices, choices.

When I fail to use my time wisely, I regret it. I have felt the sting of disappointment from a missed writing deadline or a homeschool assignment that I gave but never followed up on with one of the kids.

Have you? It may not be the internet, either. It can be a myriad of things that tempt us off course and keep us from reaching goals or finishing projects. It may be a lack of self-control in bringing order to our day and to our children. Self-control is the primary tool we use when we set priorities for each day, choosing to do those things that need to come first over things that can wait.

Guard Your Heart (and your daylight!)

Time is a gift. It really is. As my children have gotten older, I realize how quickly it goes by. I do not want to be one of those moms who looks back at my life and wishes I had redeemed the time God gave me. Instead, I want to guard it. And in order to guard my time, I have to guard my heart, making sure I am sensitive to the Lord's gentle leading and direction.

At the end of the day, self-control is like the guard over our heart. It is the gatekeeper that allows the Holy Spirit to have free reign in our hearts so that He can cultivate the other eight fruits without being hindered.

Of all the fruits of the Spirit, self-control is the determining fruit that actually allows us to accomplish all that God has for us during a particular day or season in our lives. I don't know about you, but I am so grateful for the chance to start fresh every day. Every day, we are given an opportunity to choose how we will spend our time.

> **"CHOOSE THIS DAY WHOM YOU WILL SERVE. AS FOR ME AND MY HOUSE, WE WILL SERVE THE LORD."**
> **JOSHUA 24:15**

Get A Grip! (And a good friend)

In *The Busy Homeschool Mom's Guide to Romance*, I wrote about the importance of having a true friend with whom you can share your heart. I am a huge fan of good girlfriends; they're the glue that holds me together on days when I just need someone to say, "I'm sorry you're having a bad day." At times, my girlfriends are the reality check that I need to get me back on track with my homeschooling or steer me back into a right relationship with my husband or children. They keep me from falling into the homeschool vortex by holding me accountable in many areas of my life.

I am telling you, I depend on these special women! I have several friends who, when they see me on Facebook during the day, will remind me to get back to what I am supposed to be doing! Don't you just love that? It's accountability, with a Facebook twist!

If lack of self-control is hindering you from accomplishing what God has put before you each day, let me challenge you to be real with your girlfriends about it. Ask for accountability. Seek transparency. A good friend will hold you up in prayer and hold your feet to the fire when you need her to. Don't believe that you're alone. Almost every mom I have ever known (no matter how put together she may look) has days and even seasons when self-control is a real issue.

But I Don't Even Have A Computer and I Still Can't Get Things Done!

This past month, I received a phone call from a new homeschool mom in our co-op. She was struggling with scheduling issues and, like most of us, she was trying to figure out how to have a life and still homeschool at the same time.

My first question to her was "Tell me about your internet use" and to my absolute astonishment, she informed me that they did not have access in their home to television or the internet! Now I don't know about you, but I rarely hear of people these days who don't have these modern distractions, er... conveniences. It really is unusual in the day and age we live in, but I have to say while I thought it was unusual, it was also reassuring. The internet may be new, but time management was a struggle long before its arrival on the scene.

If you're reading this thinking, "I don't have a computer and I STILL can't get things done," my hunch is that what you really need to do is learn how to best prioritize your day.

I want to direct you again to God's word. He has the answer you are looking for. Seek Him first. Even for Christians, seeking God's guidance in every day circumstances can sometimes seem to be a difficult task. As moms we are constantly distracted. It's easily the first thing we decide to forgo when our days are busy and the children need our attention. But it's the one thing we must not neglect.

"NOW SET YOUR MIND AND HEART TO SEEK THE LORD YOUR GOD." 1 CHRONICLES 22:19

Set your mind and heart to seek the Lord. It's a decision of the will. It's self-control.

Once you have gone to the Lord about what you need to do first, the rest is simply implementation and self-control. It's not really about managing time, after all. It's about managing yourself! I like to call it "me" management, because it helps remind me that the responsibility for managing the days in our home really does fall on me.

After all, the home is the domain of the woman. She sets the tone at home, by God's design. If Mama's wasting daylight, chances are, everyone else will follow suit.

Wasting Daylight? Try This: Simple Steps for Busy Homeschool Moms

Are you so busy that you're speed reading this chapter? If so, here are some key points and suggestions to help you get motivated and become intentional about how you spend your time.

🕐 If the internet is a problem for you, don't get online until after you have accomplished everything you want to do that day.

🕐 Tell your girlfriends to remind you of your goal if they see you on Facebook during the day. Some of my best reminders have come from the gentle nudges of friends who encourage me through Facebook!

🕐 Make a list each day of things you need to get done. Set a goal.

🕐 Set your phone or computer (or both) to send you text or alarm reminders to help keep you on track.

🕐 Reward yourself when you reach your goals! I like to have coffee out with my husband and talk about how things are going in our homeschool. This way we stay "on the same page" and we're better connected at home.

One of the best things about the Christian life is the knowledge that we really can do all things through Christ. If you are struggling with self-control, ask the Lord to help you. He will! His mercies are new every morning!

CHAPTER 8

Surrendered Daylight

FINDING HIS HEART FOR YOUR HOMESCHOOL

When a train goes through a tunnel and it gets dark,
you don't throw away the ticket and jump off.
You sit still and trust the engineer.
~ Corrie Ten Boom

Homeschoolers are under a lot of pressure these days.
Pressure from without …

Whether it's pressure to out-perform students in different academic environments or pressure to conform to a particular style of education or family philosophy, homeschool moms are feeling the heat.

It's easy to see the pressure from the world. After all, homeschool freedom was hard won in this country. Talk of socialization has slowed over the years as homeschoolers have entered the workforce and social spheres. Turns out, homeschooled kids are doing a pretty good job of being grownups!

These days, the pressure on homeschoolers is a little bit different than it was twenty-five years ago. I fully expect to turn on the news tomorrow and hear a story about a seven year old who has just memorized every country on the map and knows the constellations above them at any given time of year by heart. Headlines read "Homeschooled Students Excel" ... and the mom whose 5th grader is struggling with his math facts reads the article over her morning cup of tea. Slowly, subtle thoughts of inadequacy creep into her mind. "Am I doing enough? *My* son isn't doing that."

Confidence erodes as she begins to compare herself with other homeschool moms and her child with other children.

Pressure to Do More

In most areas, opportunities for homeschooling families abound: from homeschool conferences to co-ops, the sheer number of available weekly activities can make even seasoned homeschool moms dizzy.

The problem is not lack of opportunity. The problem is discerning which opportunities to take advantage of and which ones to pass up.

Now in case you didn't know, I am a huge fan of homeschool co-ops. So much so, that Jay and I founded an international ministry dedicated to helping churches start Bible teaching homeschool co-ops. However, the function of the co-op should never be to take the place of the homeschool parent. It should be to come alongside the family in support and encouragement.

Homeschool parents need encouragement! Whether you have a struggling reader or a blossoming genius on your hands, know this: God chose YOU with your child in mind. Yes, you. We serve a mighty God! He has already equipped you for the task to which you have been called.

Whether you have a struggling reader or a blossoming genius on your hands, know this: God chose YOU with your child in mind.

When I see moms struggling under the burden of other people's expectations, I cannot help but wonder if we are becoming too dependent on outside sources for homeschooling. We must not forget that it was God who called us to homeschool in the first place. He will provide what we need to homeschool our children exactly when we need it. But we must trust Him.

Like the Israelites, whom God delivered over and over again, we must remember to keep trusting Him, and not doubt His calling or His provision. Precious homeschool mom, *you are ready for the task at hand*! Whether it's beginning homeschool or algebra, you can rest assured that God will make a way. If you don't know how to teach algebra, stop worrying! Trust that God knows *exactly* how it's going to be taught.

If all the co-ops closed tomorrow, families who are being led and directed by God's spirit should and will continue to thrive in their homeschooling. This is because Christian homeschooling is now and always has been a move of the Spirit. It is about much more than academics. We must not forget that.

"I can do all things through Christ who strengthens me."

And pressure from within ...

My heart has been burdened in the past several years by what my husband and I have seen creep into the homeschool community through organizations and individuals whose well-meaning message has taken on an attitude of arrogance and self-righteousness.

Rather than depending on God, we can easily find ourselves depending on the formulas and messages of men. We hang on their every word. We dress the part. We talk the part. We take some measure of pride in following a set of rules, and we encourage others to do the same.

According to many, it's not enough to homeschool anymore. We need to wear dresses while we do it. We shouldn't put our kids in Sunday school. We shouldn't own televisions. Families who believe in courtship look down on families who don't—and vise versa.

Images of "perfect" homeschool families who live on 80 acres and grow all their own food make city dwelling homeschoolers feel like slackers. City dwellers criticize the independent spirit of homesteaders and turn up their noses toward them on blogs and through social media.

There is so much division within the homeschool community that many moms I meet are afraid to "admit" that they buy white bread on sale or that their daughters are going to college.

We are arguing over disputable matters. In Romans 14, Paul warned the church specifically NOT to do this.

We're majoring on the minors and in so doing, we

are making "minor" things into the main thing. We have unwittingly opened the door to the enemy, and as such, we are a house divided.

"IF A HOUSE IS DIVIDED AGAINST ITSELF, THAT HOUSE CANNOT STAND."
MARK 3:25

A Spiritual Battle

Do you recognize that you are in a spiritual battle? In Ephesians 6, we are told that *"We do not wrestle against flesh and blood, but against principalities. Against the spiritual forces of wickedness in dark places."*

Let's consider the term "wrestle" for a moment. The first thing I notice about this word is that wrestling is not a team sport. It's a very personal battle. In this case, it's a one-on-one battle between you and the enemy of your soul. Can you feel it?

The Bible tells us that the enemy we wrestle against does not have flesh and blood. Peter describes him as a "roaring lion" seeking someone to devour. He's not just sitting around, either. The Bible says he's "seeking" someone to devour!

Do you know who that someone is? It's you. It's your marriage

Your children. Your witness. Your life.

Whenever I speak on this topic, I like to show a picture of the lion that Peter describes in 1 Peter 5:8. This is not your run-of-the-mill lion from the zoo. This lion is hungry. This lion is mean. This lion is angry.

This is the image of the enemy of your soul. Get to know it.

Now picture this lion as the voyeur that he is. Picture him prowling around your home in the dead of night, looking in windows, listening at the door. He is watching you, looking for *any opportunity* to drive a wedge between you and your husband, between you and your teenage child. This enemy is sneaky. He will use scriptural principles to devour his enemy if he can.

Are you listening, homeschool mom? Are you watching? Are you on guard against the enemy of your soul? You need to be; because the battle you are in is for the hearts and minds of your children. A generation hangs in the balance.

Have you felt it?

Are you listening, homeschool mom? Are you watching? Are you on guard against the enemy of your soul? You need to be; because the battle you are in is for the hearts and minds of your children. A generation hangs in the balance.

Listening to the Lord

There is a passion that burns in my heart for this topic. I wrote about it in *The Busy Homeschool Mom's Guide to Romance*, too. The reason I am so passionate about personally listening to and following after God is because I have witnessed and experienced firsthand what happens when we don't.

God wants to talk with us. He longs for a personal relationship with us. He wants to encourage us and guide us, to show us where we need to shepherd our children better and to nudge us closer to our husbands in the process.

If we become so preoccupied with being the "perfect" homeschool family that we begin to follow the formulas of man rather than be guided by the Holy Spirit (both individually and as families), we *will* miss out on His heart for our families and for our homeschooling.

When we pattern ourselves after men, we are sure to miss at least part of what God would have us learn on this homeschool journey.

And *what a journey it is.* Have you noticed that homeschooling is as much about you as it is about your kids? If you haven't yet, I am betting that you will, because homeschooling is hard. (Amen?) And if we're truly in it for the Lord, it will drive us where we need to be: on our knees.

Has homeschooling brought you to your knees? If it has, that's good! Because *that is where we find the answers we really need.* That's where we'll find the freedom that God has for us. Best of all, it's where we will truly thrive: under the shadow of His wings. There is freedom and peace there!

When we recognize our freedom in Christ, the chains fall off and we begin to discover what it means to be truly free.

Romans 14 and Disputable Matters: Understanding Legalism

> "ACCEPT THE ONE WHOSE FAITH IS WEAK, WITHOUT QUARRELING OVER DISPUTABLE MATTERS."
> ROMANS 14:1

It took me a long time to recognize legalism. I think it's because I grew up in it. I lived it for so long I couldn't recognize it. As a young mother, I was as un-grace filled as anyone I knew. Maybe more. Those who did not subscribe to our particular style of parenting were looked down upon.

The company we kept encouraged us in our thinking, but eventually, several of the families who were part of our group buckled under the strain of expectations that did not come from the Lord. Families struggled under the weight.

I didn't know it then, but I've come to understand that my attitude was really *legalism*, and it's the gatekeeper of the Homeschool Vortex. Legalism says if you wear the right clothes or don't watch television, you are righteous. It judges others by an extra-biblical standard.

In grey areas such as watching TV or wearing pants versus dresses, birth control or even courtship versus dating, individuals have the freedom to make up their own mind, because these specific issues are not clearly addressed in Scripture. Legalism paves the way for pride in our own opinions instead of trusting in God's ability to lead and direct His people.

Most of the boundaries of Scripture are clearly laid out. We know that adultery for example, is sin. The Bible clearly states it. However. When a behavior, doctrine or tradition is not addressed in Scripture by a *specific* moral absolute commanding or forbidding an action, it belongs to a category of *freedom*. In areas of freedom, Christians are encouraged to establish their own convictions and are *not* permitted to judge or ridicule those who do not share them (Romans 14:3).

And while it may feel good for a while, legalism is a burdensome friend. If left unchecked, it can blind us to the sin of pride. Legalism is the opposite of freedom. It brings bondage. In recent years, legalism has plagued the homeschool community. Oh that we would be known for our love and discernment!

Moms, as soon as your *personal conviction* becomes your friend's responsibility, you have crossed into legalism. When we become dogmatic about following rules instead of following the Spirit, we are missing God's heart.

The person who is led by the Spirit, and driven by a desire to be pleasing to God, will avoid being caught up in the law. It may make us feel righteous, but in the end, when we are led by the law, legalism becomes a disguise used to cover up a failing of our flesh where discernment and love should be.

Let Love Be Your Aim

God's desire is that we would love Him with all our heart, soul, mind and strength. When we love Him in this way, we are free to follow Him with our whole heart rather than be held to the rules or the expectations of men.

> "'LOVE THE LORD YOUR GOD WITH ALL
> YOUR HEART AND WITH ALL YOUR SOUL
> AND WITH ALL YOUR STRENGTH
> AND WITH ALL YOUR MIND';
> AND, 'LOVE YOUR NEIGHBOR AS YOURSELF.'"
> LUKE 10:27

I wonder, as homeschoolers—are we loving each other? Are we known for our love of others and our grace-filled attitudes?

One of the most troubling things about legalism within the homeschool movement is that it keeps us from being totally dependent on God. As we raise our children in this way, eventually they too become bound to rules. Legalistic parents tend to raise up children who are also bound by the law. Jesus saw this in the Pharisees.

The Pharisees were known for their rules, but never for their discernment. When we teach our children to depend on a checklist of rules, there is no discernment taking place. The pharisaical mindset says "give me the law— I want the rules so I don't step out of bounds!" In doing so, we do not challenge ourselves to think through an issue to determine which biblical concepts should drive our decision making process.

There is No Formula

Where is your confidence, homeschool mom? If it's in doing things a certain way so that your kids will grow up to love and serve God, you've got to surrender. There is no formula. There is only faith.

There is no formula. There is only faith.

It's so easy to give our daylight hours to a schedule and live by a set of hard and fast rules. It's safe. But God has a much better way. His way requires a daily surrendering of our will for His, but His way bears fruit; it is not burdensome or bound by legalism.

I love the way Scripture gives a glimpse into how much God loves us! Consider what Paul said to the people at Philippi as he affirmed that if GOD began something, He would finish it. The word "confident" is a strong word … it means to be "fully persuaded or convinced" about something.

> "BEING CONFIDENT OF THIS, THAT HE
> WHO BEGAN A GOOD WORK IN YOU
> WILL CARRY IT ON TO COMPLETION
> UNTIL THE DAY OF CHRIST JESUS."
> PHILIPPIANS 1:6

Paul chose the right thing to be confident in. To completion! To completion! Don't you love that? It makes me want to sing for JOY, because some days I don't think I'll make it to grade three, let alone grade twelve! This verse reminds me that I don't need to depend on formulas or the rules of men, because I can be *confident* in God's desire to see the work He has started in me and my husband *through to completion.*

After all, it's His work. His power. His presence in our everyday lives that becomes our true source of confidence and strength as we follow Him together.

Have you surrendered your will for His?

Be confident in your ability to homeschool your kids, busy homeschool mom. Your confidence is well-placed when it is rooted in Christ and in His call on your life.

He surrendered His will to the will of the Father. He is our example.

A Surrendered Spirit

Homeschool mom, whose heart are you seeking as you plan your day? As you train and nurture your children? Choose your curriculum? Write your schedule? Before you let a speaker or an author (including me!) tell you how your day should look, whether or not it's okay to watch TV or buy store-bought bread, I encourage you to seek the Lord together with your husband. The only real way to know what God has for you each day is to ask Him.

Many homeschoolers today are forgetting that the true strength of homeschooling comes from a surrendered relationship with the living God. It's not found in a curriculum or in a program. Success will not be found in writing a wonderful schedule or planning a menu. Strength does not lie in the formulas of men. It is found in Christ alone.

I believe that when we find our strength in Christ, we will also find strength for the homeschool years. Is it hard? Yes it is! Do we ever really know what we're getting oursleves into when we obey the call of God on our lives? I don't think so!

Surrendering to God allows us to be filled with His Spirit instead of being held hostage by the opinions and directives of men. Surrender fills us with strength. Strength for the journey. Strength to finish well. Strength to be real—and strength to plan our days with confidence in *God's ability* to direct them. Are you surrendered?

I love the words of this song. It reminds me that no matter what comes, my strength, my hope, is found in Christ:

> In Christ alone my hope is found,
> He is my light, my strength, my song;
> this Cornerstone, this solid Ground,
> firm through the fiercest drought and storm.
> What heights of love, what depths of peace,
> when fears are stilled, when strivings cease!
> My Comforter, my All in All,
> here in the love of Christ I stand.
>
> by Stuart Townend and Keith Getty

"When fears are stilled, when strivings cease."

You don't have to have all the answers, Mom. He'll give them to you as you seek His heart for your life.

He's rarely early, but He's never late.

As your family grows and new challenges arise, keep

coming back to the feet of Jesus. Nurture the relationships in your home above academics. Find other women who will challenge and encourage you. Give yourself permission to fail, knowing that the work you are doing in the Lord is never in vain! Laugh at yourself. Laugh with your kids.

Be real. Be intentional.

Be surrendered.

Be HIS—and then expect His power, His provision and His presence to guide your days.

That's what makes the journey worth taking.

Contact the Author

By Mail

1400 NE 136th Avenue Ste 201

Vancouver, WA 98684

360-326-8826

www.fchm.org

On the Internet

www.heidistjohn.com

email- heidi@fchm.org

Facebook

We invite you to join other busy homeschool moms
as we laugh and talk together on Facebook!

www.facebook.com/busyhomeschoolmom

www.facebook.com/FirstClassHomeschool

Speaking

Heidi and Jay love to travel and minister to homeschool families. Heidi is available to speak at conferences, women's retreats and seminars. Her husband is a gifted worship leader and is also available to lead worship or speak at your event.

Here are a few of Heidi's most requested topics:

The Busy Homeschool Mom's Guide™ to Romance (Now in paperback!)

The Busy Homeschool Mom's Guide™ to Daylight: Time Management for the Homeschool Years

R.E.A.L. L.I.F.E. Homeschooling

Multi-Level Teaching

Homeschooling Through the Seasons of Life

The First Three Years: A Workshop for Homeschool Rookies

Lessons from Esther: Peace in Times of Fear

Notebooking and Multi-Level Teaching

10 Marriage Myths That Will Steal Your Joy

New Journaling the Homeschool Years

For Heidi's speaking schedule and for descriptions of these and other topics, visit www.heidistjohn.com

First Class Homeschool Ministries

Building Homeschool *Communities* around the World!

Focusing on the Things of First Importance
1 Corinthians 15:3,4

Biblical Training
Proven Framework
Start-up Kit
Co-op Website

Membership Database
Leadership Support
Member Benefits
Promotion

Class Ideas
Training

Over 40 locations across North America!

Request a **FREE**
information pack at:

www.firstclasshomeschool.org

360.326.8826